The House that God Built

The story of Meadgate Church
as recalled and compiled by

Doris Hill
and friends

The House that God Built
Copyright © Doris Hill
Feb 2015

2nd Edition

Published by Philos Publishing
www.philos.org.uk

Philos Publishing

All rights reserved. No part of this publication may be reproduced, stored in a retrieval system, or transmitted in any form or by any means, electronic, mechanical, photocopying or otherwise, without the prior written consent of the author.

Short extracts may be used for teaching purposes or encouraging people as part of expressing the good news of Jesus and the Kingdom of heaven.

A CIP catalogue record of this title
is available from the British Library

Printed by Lightning Source

ISBN 978-0-9572704-2-8

Contents

Chapter	Heading	Page
	Contents	i
	Map of Meadgate Area	ii
	Acknowledgements	iii
	Prefaces	v
1.	The Mustard Seed Time	1
2	At Meadgate School	5
3.	A Church with a Building	11
4.	The Building	33
5.	Progress of the Church	39
6.	Notable Events	45
7.	Features of the Meadgate Fellowship	51
8.	Music	59
9.	Artefacts and Memorabilia	63
10.	Publications	75
11.	Testimonies	79
12.	Time Line	119

Appendices

| A | Foundational Documents | 145 |

Map of Meadgate Area

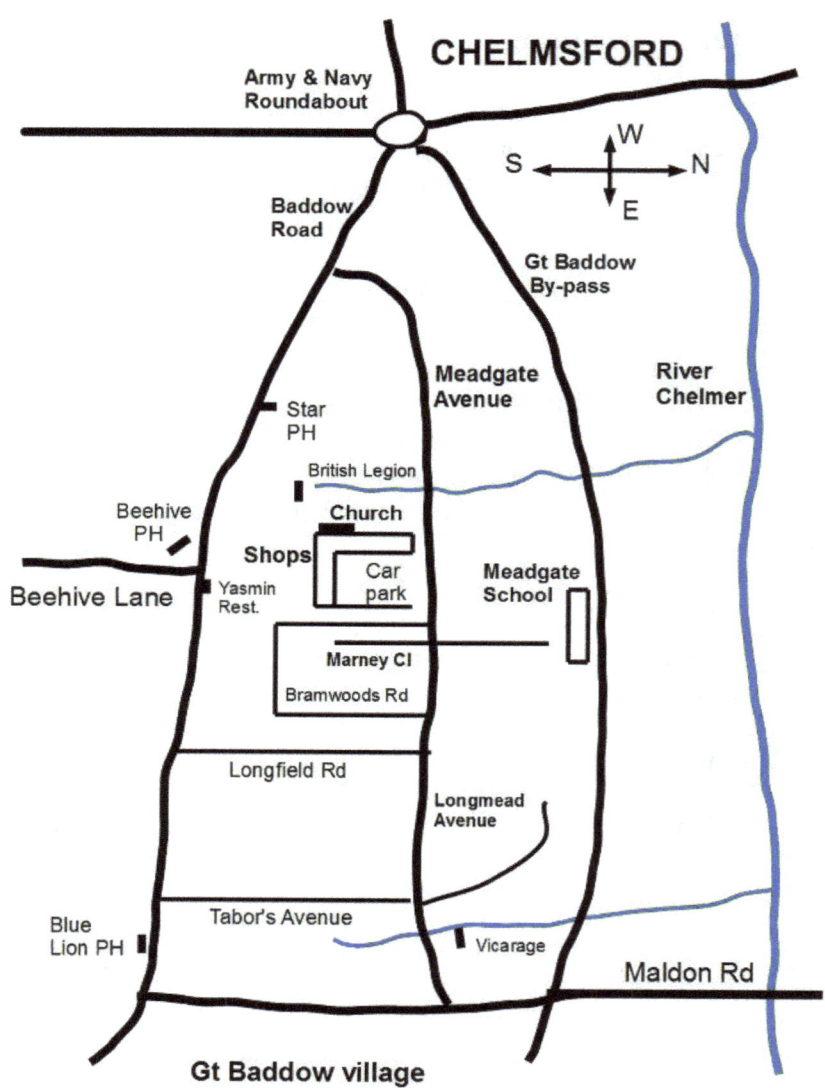

Map of Meadgate Area

Acknowledgements

I have been greatly blessed by all the help I have received in putting this account together in the way of practical help, encouragement, interest, time given to help me and the faith that my fellow brothers and sisters in Christ have had in me.

Thank you so much to all those who have responded to my request for their private testimonies. I'm sure they will add further interest to the reading of this book.

My words will not convey how much I appreciate Melvyn Sach. He has spent many hours looking up from his records all the things I have asked of him. I truly believe that he is the one who has put most of this book together, because I have used so much of what he has researched for me. I just happen to be good at typing. When I consider all he has done, I realise how much faith he had in me to do all that. He encouraged me every step of the way. He has been greatly used by God in the producing of this book. God must have had him in mind when he was conceived and made him a hoarder of church documents and paraphernalia. May God bless him richly, for his service to Him.

My grateful thanks to Allan Bell who when told by Bill that I was burdened because, looking ahead, I didn't know what to do with my writings once I had finished. Allan took that burden away because he had the expertise and took pity on me. He has been very patient in teaching me how to do things. He has been a real friend indeed and in need. The Lord bless and keep you Allan.

Whilst I was at a bus stop one day, I happened to meet Leslie Ventham and told her that I was going to write a book about the history of Meadgate. Leslie had had a thought about writing a book also, and she said now she wouldn't have to do it. However she gave me the title. It witnessed to me straight away that that was the perfect name for my book. I had been going to call it "The History of Meadgate Church". Leslie's title was just perfect as I truly want to give Glory to God because he brought the church into being. Thank you so much Leslie and also thank you for your encouragement and enthusiasm about the book.

Our previous Curates and present Vicar have all encouraged me and were all willing to be involved in the history of this church and have all said it was a special time for them and how much they loved the fellowship they had with us. They have all given me encouragement. May God bless them with peace, joy and happiness in Him.

Pat Davies has also encouraged me as she searched out the artefacts and features of the church. This was a great help to me as her memory is better than mine and also it saved me time having to find out for myself. I am truly thankful to her for her time and encouragement.

Now my hope and prayer is that the newer generations will take up the mantle and continue with the wonderful "The House That God Built" story for the sake of future generations should the Lord delay His coming. It means keeping records of all kinds so that God's continuing plan will be recorded.

All Praise to His wonderful Name.

Prefaces

Preface by the Bishop of Chelmsford

'The House that God Built'

This delightful and lovingly-written history of Meadgate church takes the church back to its roots. It will remind all who come after, of the foundations that are being built on today. Meadgate has been a living parable since its inception. It began as a mustard seed and now fully grown is a space where others find welcome. In the Gospels, Jesus asks, 'What is the Kingdom of God like? What shall I compare it to? It is like a mustard seed, which a man took and planted in his garden. It grew and became a tree and the birds of the air perched in its branches'. And that reflects something of the Kingdom life and witness of Meadgate church.

I am grateful to Doris Hill and friends of Meadgate for writing this book. Over the years Meadgate has welcomed young and old; encouraged, affirmed, discipled and sent many out in mission. And we need to remind ourselves that we are all here because of the faithfulness of those who were before us, and that we all play our part in leaving a legacy - a missional church. At a time when we celebrate the centenary of the Chelmsford diocese we need to offer back our history with thanks and embrace God's future for us!

Mones and Sally Farah are in a significant line of ministers at Meadgate over the last 50 years, but under their wise leadership, pastoral prowess, and inspired teaching many have come to a deeper and fuller maturity in Christ. And I thank them for their share with me in the ministry.

The Rt. Revd Stephen Cottrell
The Bishop of Chelmsford

Preface by the Author

I've always realised that God had a Master Plan for the Meadgate area from almost the beginning of my life in this area.

It began with the proposed building of the estate and the Revd Jack Kingham, rector of St Mary's, finding out about it. As soon as he heard about the plans, he began praying for the planting of a church, and he also made enquiries as to whether there would be a site for a church building. He was informed that there was and that he would have the option of building on it, providing it was built within five years; otherwise the option would be offered to another religious body, whoever would be interested in it.

The site was to be where the Brookbank flats for the elderly now stand. Obviously no other religious party was able to build on it so hence Brookbank. Jack was the first one to be offered the site and then when he failed to build on it because of funds, Jack passed it on to the Roman Catholic church who had the option also for five years and it would then have gone to the Church of the Latter Day Saints, but they had already began their church in Baddow Road. Eventually the council stepped in and the Brookbank flats were built.

It all began just over a year ago when I awoke in the night and my instant thought was Meadgate Church, and then I heard "write a book". I couldn't get back to sleep wondering what it meant. Then I said "Well Lord if you want me to do this then keep this in my mind or show me to let go of it." I couldn't let go of it.

I knew that I was ill equipped to take on this (to me) huge task and prayed long and hard that as I was to do it God would go ahead of me, lead me and help me. I was also aware that I am the only one still at the church 50 years on who was at the very beginning of God's plan for a church here on the estate, so I had to cast my mind back and try to remember how it happened.

I found that my memory was clear about the events as they happened, but not so clear about the names of those who soon became involved. Therefore I have to believe that they know who they are and God knows who they are and if I've missed out anyone I pray they will forgive me and understand that it was so long ago. However I well know the lovely friends who shared the first Sunday school with me and their subsequent service to get the church off the ground, albeit without a building. I like to think of it as a church without walls (think I borrowed that phrase from somewhere, but I like it).

As I began work on this book, I had thoughts that most churches have a wonderful history and that we should have a history, something for future generations to be able to look back on. God must have the glory for this story because this church exists today because of his master plan for us and for future generations. We gladly give God the Glory for we have all benefited as a fellowship.

There are twelve chapters in this book because my grand-daughter Katie Hart was struck by the significance of the number twelve in our family (two of our homes in the past years have been number twelve's) and at the time of writing this we just happen to have twelve grand-children; and of course Our Lord appointed twelve apostles.

It is obvious to me that all who have passed through this church have truly been blessed as are we who fellowship here today. It has been and will be our church family with so much love and caring among us. My own life would have been empty without this family to which I belong.

All glory and praise to our God and Father and His Son Jesus Christ for all He has done.

Doris Hill, 2013

The dates, times and names in this account of the 'House that God Built' have been gleaned from all the records that could be found. In addition people provided these sort of details from their memories. It may be that there are some errors particularly in the exact timescale with regard to dates and times. Please let the author know of any such errors and they will be incorporated into a later edition of the book.

Chapter 1
The Mustard Seed Time

In the beginning, the Revd Jack Kingham, the then vicar of St. Mary's church in Great Baddow, heard about an estate that was planned for the Meadgate area of his parish. This began a desire in him to plant a church on the estate and he began praying that this would happen in order that the people who would inhabit the houses on the estate would be served and hear of the salvation that Jesus was offering to all who would accept Him into their lives.

God heard his prayers and so the way began to open for a church to be built. My husband Bill, myself and our two children, moved onto the Meadgate estate as Bill had began a new job in Chelmsford and our search for a house led us to Meadgate and to a house in Marney Close.

Up until this time, Bill hadn't been too happy about me being a Christian and there was tension between us, but I had been a Sunday school teacher where we had lived in Shotgate near Wickford and I still wanted to carry on this work for God. First I had to find a church and St. Mary's was where I chose to go.

I spoke to a new neighbour who had also just moved in and told her that I wanted to go to St. Mary's for 8 am communion and felt a bit nervous about it. She said she would come with me. Her name is Norma Monk, so we went together and were welcomed by the Revd Jack Kingham.

The Mustard Seed Time

My next need was to find a Sunday school for my two children. Because of my family situation, it was going to be a bit difficult for me to be committed to every Sunday morning and I couldn't send Peter and Jenny to either St. Mary's or St. Paul's on their own because of main roads.

The thought entered my head that I could teach Sunday School at home. When I approached Bill about the idea, much to my surprise he was quite open to the idea. I then approached Jack Kingham and he was over the moon about it and said that he would keep it in mind, but there would need to be a superintendent in authority over the project. He continued to converse with me and had a plan he told me.

In 1963 a young newly- married couple (the Gilders) moved onto the Meadgate estate. Both of them were teachers and Christians. Jack got together with them and our first date for Sunday school was planned. During the time when this was being worked out, I became pregnant with our third child and my father was taken ill with cancer and didn't have long to live.

Jeff was born six weeks early, but then my father came to live with us so that I could look after him.

The first Sunday school class was hosted in my neighbour Norma's home and we continued there until I was free to take over. We started with just two children: Trevor and Karen Walden.

1960's Doris Hill at the back door of her Meadgate home greets the Sunday School children waiting on her garden path

The Mustard Seed Time

My children, Peter and Jenny, if I remember rightly, were both unwell on that first opening day so they were not to be at the first class, which I was disappointed about, but I was so pleased to get started. Terry and Beryl Gilder were our lay leaders and it was such an exciting time.

My father passed away the first week in November and from then on Sunday school took place as was originally planned in our house.

Meadgate Estate was completely built by then and there were lots of young families now living in the area. Every house was visited by Jack Kingham and his curate and parents were invited to send their children to the new Sunday School.

When we moved the Sunday School to our house we began to meet in the hall. Then after a talk by Terry, we went into the lounge to have our lesson and do some activity. Each week our numbers increased as the news spread. Terry decided to break a 78's gramophone record on the Sundays when attendance increased, and that happened every Sunday.

Beryl Gilder and sitting room pupils settling down to lessons in Doris Hill's house.

The Mustard Seed Time

Eventually we had so many children that we were using every room in the house. On top of that we started a family service once a month and it was held in our bedroom (which was the largest room in the house). Percy Walden (Father of Trevor and Karen) offered to help us get the room ready. It meant taking our bed apart and clearing the room in order to put chairs out.

Richard and Adrienne Wilson offered to open their home for the older group of children and so Sunday school was happening in two homes. After a while, with the increase in the numbers of children, we needed more space.

Terry decided to ask the council if we could hire the school hall. Permission was given and the Sunday School moved into the School on April 23rd 1967.

Chapter 2
At Meadgate School

The number of children increased rapidly. In fact we now had more than 100 children and we had about 15 teachers. There was John Bayliss on loan from Elim church. He later emigrated to New Zealand to be with family. Sheila Southgate, Louise Wright, Margaret Brett (nee Wright), Jean Bass, Jean Sach, Melvyn Sach (who later became superintendent and leader of the older group, with myself (Doris Hill) leading the younger group. There was Marjorie Thorne, Alison Newman and Margaret Tapp (and I'm sure there were some others but regret that I cannot remember them all).

Meadgate Primary School provided the Sunday School/Church with Sunday accommodation in its premises from 1967 to 1973

It was a wonderful time. In the summer we were able to take tables and chairs outside for our classes. We began to have family services once a month in the school and we soon had lots of parents attending this service. After the departure of Terry and Beryl, Melvyn took over as Sunday school Superintendent.

It was arranged that he would lead the junior group and that I would lead the infant group. If I remember rightly, John Bayliss took on the older children, and so we continued until the church was up and running.

At Meadgate School

It became very obvious that we needed to have our own church building and in 1965 the Revd David Evans, St Mary's curate, had begun looking at various sites. Whilst this was happening other events were taking place. We now had our own curate in the person of the Revd Michael Stedman.

The First Curate

The Revd Michael Stedman came to us in 1968 and immediately set to work getting involved with all that was already going on. I remember he called a meeting with all of us to get a full picture of how we were operating, and he gave us a talk about the responsibilities of teaching. If I remember correctly he based his talk on 1 Timothy 4:16. It caused me to feel a bit scared as I realised the tremendous responsibility we were undertaking, but that talk stayed with me all the years that I was teaching these children. No doubt he was having meetings with all the other groups.

Monthly morning services were held at the home of Melvyn and Jean Sach. Bible studies also took place in their home. Monthly evening services were held in the home of Pat and Olwyn Kerrison and occasionally in the Common Room at Tusser Court by kind permission of the warden. Also a young wives group (now called CAMEO) had started.

More and more people became involved and gradually from a small beginning a Church came into existence and continued to grow. The mustard seed had taken root and was growing.

It was obvious that at some point there would be a church building and therefore there had to be fund raising. A senior citizens group (as it was then called) met in the home of Miss North where they knitted and crocheted for this purpose. We began to have rummage sales and then many others came up with ideas to raise money. Wives group collected green shield stamps, (a thing of the past). You collected these stamps when you shopped at certain shops and when you had many of them you could redeem items from these shops according to how many you collected. My husband Bill used them for buying petrol and I once collected a whole tea service an item at a time.

We had a mini walk and a very successful fete on the school playing field. Donations kept coming from various sources.

Springfield Park Church gave us money. Other gifts apart from money were given. We received Bibles, an alms dish and a lectern. Money was made by collecting newspapers and Mr and Mrs Keeble took on the buy a brick scheme.

At Meadgate School

Michael and Gill Stedman had come to us following the departure of David and Rita Evans. Michael and Gill have submitted an account of events leading up to the building of the new church for which I am truly thankful to them. It is included in this book as they wrote it (Chapter 12). It must have been a real test of their memories as it was so long ago.

The Revd Jack Kingham now planned the first committee and I was invited to be on it which was a bit daunting for me but I soon got into the planning of various things. This committee consisted of people who were qualified to deal with all the rules and regulations and by-laws and who knew who were the people to contact in the Borough Council. They drew up plans which they submitted and we began to search the Meadgate area for a suitable site. Several sites were suggested and looked into, but there was always the problem of car parking and other obstacles were in the way. Eventually the site we now have was the one that we proceeded with.

At the committee meetings it was discussed how the building was to be used for community purposes as well as a place of worship and it was then decided that we should have a playgroup. It was no co-incidence that Betty Mead had just trained as a Playgroup leader. God had his plan and it was evolving.

Somewhere around this time, Terry Gilder saw the need for the people on the Meadgate estate to be informed of the plan to build a church and so it was planned to invite people to a meeting at the school and tell them of the plans. This was very well attended and Terry gave a really good talk. People from the community showed a keen interest and were very encouraging

The mustard seed was beginning to sprout. Michael Stedman produced an account of what was happening at the time and put it on overhead projector slides with the title: "The Mustard Seed". Michael was a very busy man at this point. He had a church to look after even though we didn't have a building and also he was very involved in the planning as well. We must be very thankful to him and to God for sending him to us. He was the man for the moment.

In 1972 the following article appeared in the Great Baddow Parish Life magazine:

> 'Meadgate church enters 1972 full of expectation. We see in the Meadgate area distinction between the church as a church and the church as a building. The Meadgate church has existed in some form or another since 1963. It was reckoned that by 1973 the building would be completed, but it was completed earlier than expected. The opening dedication service was held on 18 June 1972.'

At Meadgate School

Let us briefly review the stages in the church's development so far, using the metaphor of the seed as we did in our Meadgate filmstrip "A Grain of Mustard Seed".

The seed was sown a long time ago by God in the hearts of people on the estate. In 1963 it produced its first shoot, the beginning of a Sunday School. Since that date a Wives Group and Darby and Joan club had been formed. Overflowing Family Services had been held in Meadgate School, groups had met in houses for Bible Study and Sunday Worship and perhaps most moving of all, there had been occasional House Communions.

I can't remember all the details of the plans which were presented to the Borough Council, or the conditions we had to observe but there were lots of letters going to and fro. Brian Newman is the only person left that I know who could help, so I contacted him, but like me he doesn't have any recollection. It was so long ago. I do recall that there was concern about money and that St. Mary's helped by a loan and there were some other loans offered. So we started off in debt and we had to carry on with our fund raising.

There was a photograph taken of some of the members of the already-in-existence church at the building site behind Meadgate shops. I remember that Bill and I arrived too late to be in it. I was so disappointed.

A.N Hill was appointed to build the church and the date was set for him to begin. I was very excited and visited the site often during its erection.

On one occasion whilst I was watching one of the bricklayers, I asked him if I could lay a brick to which he replied "Of course you can". The brick I laid is one at the back of the prayer room, which is also now used for a crèche. It was really exciting watching the progress. Eventually it was completed.

In the meantime we had to think about chairs, Bibles, Prayer book, alms dish, and communion vessels. These were provided by various people. We were told there were many chairs in the house next door to Thompson's TV shop in the village, but that we would have to go and collect them. Terry, Beryl, Bill and I collected them but they were covered with spiders' webs and quite dirty, so we had to set to and clean them. We had some willing volunteers to help us.

Everything was coming together. God was working among us and to Him we give all the Glory. He heard Jack Kingham's prayers and was answering them. He brought all the people with the skills and know-how at the right time and it was all working to His plan.

At Meadgate School

We were already a church in action, just awaiting a central place to worship and it was coming together. It had taken a long time but we knew it would not be long before we had our own church, our own place of worship.

As for me, well I had not an iota of an idea that was what God intended. My plans had not gone beyond my desire to have a few Sunday school children round to my house to teach them about Jesus along with my own two, Peter and Jenny, and later Jeff.

I have managed to do some research among early magazines, which would have been impossible if Melvyn Sach had not hoarded them all these years. He kindly sorted them out and let me have them. All the details that I found will be in the "Time Line" (Chapter 12). I was glad to have gone through them because it brought back a lot of memories.

Chapter 3
A Church with a Building

The time came when we were able to move into the new church building and then all the purposes of the building were now in evidence. Playgroup began under the leadership of Betty Mead, and that was highly successful for the needs of young families on the estate. Wives group, senior citizens (as they were then called), committee meetings, Sunday school and of course Morning and Evening services.

There were problems of course. We had so many Sunday school children, that we found the church hall really not big enough and we began to lose them gradually. Another problem was that we had to have Sunday school at an earlier time than the service, which was very inconvenient for parents who were church members because they had to bring their children for the first hour and then keep them in the service with them at the next hour. They would bring the children and then go home and have to come back again. After a time we were mostly left with children who had Christian parents who were church members. This was really sad as we lost so many children from the estate. This also meant that there was no need for all of the teachers, although some of them were only on loan to us until the church was built. We have to acknowledge their support for the years they were with us in the school and we were truly thankful to them.

Church life had now truly began. As we were a Church of Ecumenical Experiment (which meant that we welcomed all believers irrespective of their denomination) certain issues arose, for instance, the style of communion we would use. Should we use the chalice or individual little glasses? I believe that our curate Michael Stedman had to see the Bishop regarding that issue, but in the end for a while we used both in turn.

Michael had appointed his committee and there was much planning to do, but again we had very able and competent people with their various skills to do it. Bill (my husband) was on the committee and his skills at DIY came in very useful. He was commissioned to produce various pieces of furniture that were needed to keep things tidy. And he often became involved in decision making.

So according to my failing memory that is how it all began, but the mustard seed continues to grow.

After Michael and Gill moved to Norfolk to take up Michael's post as a vicar, the church was then in a time of interregnum and was led by Terry Gilder and a team of deacons.

A Church with a Building

During this period the opportunity was taken to renovate the curate's house at 55 Longfield Road. The kitchen was re-designed and a new cooker and central heating were installed. Bill then organised a team of willing helpers from the church to decorate the house.

The Second Curate

Our new curate, the Revd Tony Bishop and his wife Pat together with their one year old twin boys Jonathon and Christopher moved into the house during August 1973. Tony took his first service at Meadgate on Sunday 26th August.

Tony was highly qualified and had two degrees to his name: M.A and M.Th. Under his leadership some changes were introduced, one of which was the pattern and form of Holy Communion services. As from January 1974 the third Sunday of the month was to be the Holy Communion service at 11.15 am. Up to then we had had only two Holy Communion services a month: 8.00 am and 7.00 pm For the elderly, particularly in the winter months this was unsuitable. The newly introduced 11.15am on the third Sunday proved to be a more suitable time.

Another change was the introduction of a new service called "Series Three" in place of the "Eucharist for the Seventies" previously used. This brought Meadgate into line with St. Mary's and St. Paul's and an ever increasing number of churches all over the country, and was in modern language.

Tony worked hard as he settled in the church and got to know the people. It couldn't have been easy balancing church duties and giving time to his young family. Also it must have been such hard work for Pat having to manage the very young twins and being a support to Tony. However the church fellowship gave what support they could as we all moved forward together under our new leadership with the diaconate.

Pat was very involved in the running of Cameo, which was then called "The Young Wives Group".

In 1974 the original Meadgate Committee was disbanded. This committee had guided the church in its early days of formation and it had fulfilled its function before the appointment of Deacons. They had accomplished a great deal during this time.

The Diaconate's elected members according to records were :- Mr C Abbott (Treasurer), Mrs M Barton (Secretary), Mrs M Bishop, Mr T Gilder, Mr W Hill and Mr M Sach.

A Church with a Building

Family services were held on the first Sunday morning of every month and started introducing dramatic presentation instead of a talk. Melvyn Sach and Clive Abbott presented the first two and they were an instructive and entertaining way of presenting the truth of the Bible.

1970's Sunday Service - A dramatic presentation

Tony and the leadership looked at the possibility of a visitation programme. The idea was to visit every house on the estate backed up by prayer and follow up where appropriate.

In May 1974 Bill Hill (with help) completed a chalet in the garden of the curate's house, which was to be used as a quiet study for Tony and it proved invaluable away from the hustle and bustle of the house. Besides which it was more convenient for Tony to be able to minister to those who needed his help.

In the meantime, fellowship meetings were at this time being held every Thursday at 8pm in the house of Pat and Eddie Davies at 56 Longfield Road.

In the July of 1974, Percy Walden and his wife Joyce agreed to take on the job of caretaking at the church centre. Percy had been with Bill and I almost from the beginning and we are so grateful to God for all the help and support he had given us. We missed him terribly when he went to be with the Lord quite suddenly in June 1978. His wife Joyce provided the lectern with an inscribed plaque in his memory, and it is still in the church and still very much used. Joyce carried on with the job of caretaking with the help of church members who were on the rota.

A Church with a Building

During Tony's ministry, he and Jack Kingham with their committees arranged for a team of twelve student ministers, called "In the Name of Jesus" to spend two weeks sharing their faith and teaching us more about the gifts of the Spirit. For me and my family it was a very special time in our lives. We were very blessed and learned much from their ministry.

An additional blessing for us was that we were privileged to be host and hostess to Graham Kendrick who was at that time writing many of the new worship songs which we still sing from time to time. We hadn't realised quite how famous he was to become later. When we were asked to host him, Tony Bishop told us he was well known and many people told us that we were blessed to have him. He had already produced an LP entitled 'Paid on the Nail'. He held a concert at what is now the cinema. He fitted in so well with our family and would spend many hours ministering to us and praying for us. As a result of our friendship, we were invited to his wedding to Jill in Wolverhampton. Since that time we have seen him at several events such as Spring Harvest and at the March for Jesus.

Tony and family left us on 2nd January 1977 and after training for missionary work they left for Nigeria where Tony took up a post in a theological college. Another era had ended in Meadgate.

The March for Jesus was a very memorable event for us as a church as many of us decided to represent our church on the march. We made much preparation for this, like making banners to let onlookers know where we came from and our own personal preparations with food, drinks, umbrellas and ways to cope with the children and their needs. It was absolutely exhilarating.

Melvyn helped me to put together the events of the happenings whilst Tony and Pat were with us and he found a tribute to them in the 1977 January Magazine. It reads as follows:-

"The people of Meadgate Church have shared the ministry of Rev Tony Bishop through a period of consolidation and Tony was God's well-chosen man for the job. Tony came to us as a proven scholar. Whilst the Parish at large was able to use his learning in the Lay Readership Training scheme, the people of Meadgate found they had a minister whose preaching was always authoritative, sound and clear. Tony's mind was also applied to the task of organising and planning the general programme of activities which is Meadgate Church. The process of consolidation has inevitably involved innovation, another ability which Tony displayed in good measure. Notable innovations during Tony's stay have been: the introduction of Series Three Holy Communion, Family Worship, Meeting Point, informal worship, Midweek Services, Toddler's club, Family Time and a number of routine activities vital to the function and witness of Meadgate Church".

A Church with a Building

"In all these developments, Tony has worked willingly with the deacons and with other church committees and organizations. He has accepted and used other peoples' good ideas, and he has charitably been prepared to amend or abandon plans of his own in consultation with those with whom he has worked.

Pat, who was a member of the Wives Group committee, and the boys, have played their part in the fellowship of the church. A notable family occasion was the arrival of baby Dominic in June 1976.

We shall miss the family as much as Tony, but we join with the people of the Parish in wishing them God's richest blessings in the future, both in their ministry and as a family."

A very fitting tribute I thought as I came to terms with my own feelings of loss. However as I often say to myself "All things come to pass." So at the end of 1976 it was carry on the work of the Lord and look forward to our next incumbent, and during the time of waiting the church was led by a Diaconate comprising of Terry Gilder (Vice Chairman), Clive Abbott, Mary Barton, Marion Bishop, Bill Hill and Melvyn Sach.

The Third Curate

The Revd John Adams was welcomed as Curate of Meadgate Church in February 1977 together with his wife Anna. They had been married just over four years and had moved around during that time working for the Protestant Churches in Western Europe. They came looking forward to a settled period of ministry in Baddow.

In the April of that year, Terry and Beryl moved to Suffolk where Terry was to take up the position of Headmaster in a local school there. It was a very sad time for me and to others I expect, but an opportunity that they both felt was right for them at that time. So we said Goodbye to them as a family. We missed the children also:- David, Lucy and Philip. After their departure Melvyn Sach was elected as Vice Chairman. Our treasurer was then Clive Abbott and Church Secretary Mary Barton. The vacancy left on the Diaconate through the loss of Terry Gilder was filled by Tom Smith-Hughes.

The Revd Tony Bishop and his wife Pat had left a thriving and growing church and John Adams relished the challenge set before him. He came to a church with strong emphasis on families, of a thriving playgroup, Sunday School, Pathfinders, Wayfinders, Wives Group and a strong Senior citizens group. In addition there were House groups.

John and Anna set to work very much as a team and soon became a familiar sight around Meadgate often with their little Dachshund dog who seemed to share in most activities. Another feature was their white Renault car, the old "sit up and beg" type.

A Church with a Building

John was very efficient and organised and liked things to be done properly. Anna worked closely with him adding her ever calm and cool influence. He was very keen on evangelism and he had a heart for Mission. His preaching was therefore always Bible based and Gospel centred. His great hobby and passion was music. He had a harpsichord which I believe he built himself. He had built more than one. Anna was also musical and played a few wind instruments. It was no surprise then when in December 1977 John put forward the idea of forming a music group. Russ Cooper was the right person to bring this about and so he did. I remember my husband Bill was really enthusiastic about playing his guitar in the group John being the thorough person that he was, worked his musicians to a high standard. I think maybe Jean Sach was probably a bit relieved by this new group as she had been the only pianist we had had from the beginning and had faithfully played at nearly all the services since the church was built.

In the church magazine July 1977 following a Sunday afternoon with his deacons, John Adams outlined his vision for the future.

1 The building up of the local fellowship of the church.

2 <u>Visiting</u>:- In an effort to get to know each other, each Deacon would have responsibility for so many members each.

3 <u>Healing</u>:- It was felt that the church still had a ministry of healing both physical and spiritual and the Lord's will needed to be found as to how to fulfil this ministry.

4 <u>Training</u>:- It was stressed how important was the need for training and equipping people to perform any job in the church to which they felt called. This applied particularly to church leaders, Sunday school teachers, House groups leaders and any who wanted to learn more.

5 <u>Bible study and Prayer groups</u>:-   There were several groups meeting but it was felt that there needed to be more cohesion and common purpose among them. One idea was for fortnightly House groups to alternate with a church based Bible study and Prayer meeting.

6 <u>Sunday worship</u>:- The need to work towards a situation where the whole church family could meet at the same time each Sunday.

7 <u>Youth</u>:- There was general satisfaction at the Sunday school although there was the need for more leaders in the Pathfinders. Starting in September, they were to have all their activities on a weekday evening for a trial period.

8 <u>Finance</u>:- Our income through offerings and envelopes was £1800 for 1976 which is approximately £35 per week. In the three months January to March 1977 to when John and Anna Adams arrived, weekly income was £39.

A Church with a Building

John Adams was later to lead the church into another important change in September 1977. Up to then, because of the restricted size of the church building, we had to have two lots of meetings on a Sunday morning. Sunday school was at 10.00am, and the morning service at 11.15am. Because numbers of children had dropped compared with previous years, it was decided to implement an all age Sunday morning pattern at 10.00am every Sunday. The familiar Family Service would still happen on the first Sunday of the month, with the whole church family remaining together. On other Sundays, the pattern would be as for Family worship, which meant everyone starts worship together, then the children split up into their own teaching and activity groups in the various side rooms. This was an important change that enabled all family ages to be present on a Sunday morning at the same time. In addition to the above, the evening service was changed from 7.00pm to 6.30pm.

John's first year with us was one of steady growth and encouragement. The annual report covering the period March 1977 to March 1978 reported much to be grateful to God for.

Worship:- The major change in September with the new pattern of Sunday morning services was going well although a few children had been lost who didn't take to the new system. The introduction of family communion on the fifth Sunday of each month had proved worthwhile.

Music:- The new music group had made an encouraging start, and it's singers and instrumentalists were involved in a number of services. Congregational singing was usually lively and new worship songs and hymns were introduced.

Leadership:- One of the exciting things in the life of the church was the sharing of leadership. Many members worked hard, preaching, helping with the services, planning activities and helping those in need.

Finance:- A big step forward in 1977 was the completion of all outstanding debts on the church building. This helped the Parish and Diocese who had been heavily subsidising us.

Church and Young People:- They played a huge part in the development of the church. It hadn't been easy to accept the changes resulting from the new Sunday morning pattern, but we had felt the Lord was calling us to change, and that it would benefit the whole church.

A Church with a Building

The Pathfinders too experienced change in September, moving all activities including Bible teaching to Tuesday evenings with average attendance 35. In September a Wayfinders group was formed from the older Pathfinder girls. Teaching was on Sunday evenings with occasional weekly activities as well as visits to other groups.

Wives group (later called CAMEO) was very well attended once a fortnight with a varied programmer There was much emphasis on Community care and Handicrafts. There was also a fortnightly Bible discussion group.

Senior Citizens continued to grow with a varied weekly programme. An exciting time was had at the old peoples welfare handicraft exhibition when the club won the cup for second prize. We were sad to lose the Chairman Jan Collins who had moved away. Grateful thanks were extended to Dorothy Bradley for stepping into the Chairman's shoes.

Playgroup:- The Playgroup started 1977 with a drop in numbers but vacancies were gradually filled throughout the year. The Queen's Silver Jubilee was celebrated by the children with parties at the end of May and an open evening for parents in July.

Toddler's Club:- 1977 was a year of growth with numbers during the year almost doubling. This group was seen not just as a valuable opportunity for parents and toddlers, but as a means of sharing the good news of Jesus Christ.

Curate's Postscript

At the end of his first year the Revd John Adams wrote the following in the church magazine April 1978:-

> "At the end of our first year at Meadgate, we thank God for all He has shown us, and for our fellowship in the gospel with those who so soon became real friends. Thank you for your welcome and your willingness to work with us for God. We look forward with confidence that the Lord has great things in store for all, and plenty of work for us to do."

John and Anna continued with us until March 1980. Their three years with us were eventful with steady growth and strong leadership. John worked closely with his elders Melvyn Sach and Bill Hill with whom he met regularly and together with the Meadgate Committee the church ran with a high degree of mutual co-operation and common endeavour. John and Anna never lost their concern for Europe and their calling to return to that theatre led to their leaving us.

A Church with a Building

Their last Sunday was 30th March 1980 when a full church heard Melvyn say how much we would miss their combined leadership and personal fellowship. The speaker was Mr Stuart Harris, President of the European Christian Mission to which John and Anna had been called.

We were indeed sorry to see them go but sent them out with our blessing and prayers together with gifts and a bouquet of flowers. We had had such fun times with John and Anna. We had social events in which we would have entertainments. We would do comedy sketches and different kinds of shows. We had such talent among us to make us laugh and have fun. We always had New Year parties ending with seeing the old year out and the new year in and leaving us with wonderful feelings of togetherness.

It was during their curacy that my daughter Jenny told us she was going to be married. At that time she was working in Florida as a Nanny. Her fiancé, Jim, had to return to America, his homeland, so that is why Jenny got the job, to be near him. From there Jenny phoned to say she was coming home to be married in six weeks' time. This threw me into a panic as I didn't know where to begin to prepare. I spoke to Marion Bishop about my anxiety and she said "Don't worry, we'll begin a committee and make plans." To cut a long story short, it was a wonderful wedding because nearly everyone in the church was involved and so many took on a specific job. I was told not to do anything, just enjoy it. John was going to marry them and when they were both back in the UK John and Anna had Jim to stay with them together with his brother and Jenny of course with us. John performed the ceremony and in such a special way as if we were members of his own family. He made a tape recording of it and gave us a copy. Bill and I were overwhelmed by the love given by our church fellowship and all their efforts.

The Fourth Curate/First Team Vicar

With the departure of John and Anna, we were once more in a period of interregnum and this time we were led through this phase by Melvyn Sach and Bill Hill.
During this period, our thoughts turned to getting the curate's house ready for our next incumbent. We had always known that the house in Longfield Road was inadequate as a dwelling for a curate with a family. Men of the ministry always need a study, and at that time what should have been an ideal place for a study downstairs was being used as a bedroom. At some point it was decided that the house should be extended and so it was. Two more bedrooms for the upstairs plus a bathroom and shower unit. This having been accomplished, we had a decent home for the next incumbent.

A Church with a Building

It made us feel so sorry that our previous Curates had had to manage as it was. After this was done then a team of workers from our fellowship set to and decorated and painted. It was such an improvement and we thank God that we had been able to do it. Because of this I have since then felt that it is so important for a clean and nicely decorated home be part of our welcome to our new incumbents.
Our next curate was Peter Nicholson, accompanied by his lovely wife Diane and their two daughters Sarah and Tracey. I was quite impressed that Peter had been in the RAF and I don't think I was the only one. We welcomed them with joy as it was obvious that they were a very friendly warm family. During their time with us, not only did we appreciate their fellowship and caring for us all but also that there was an expectation that God was leading us into a new period of growth.

Since I had been involved in Sunday School teaching from the very beginning, it was with great excitement to me that we were going to have our own Sunday School rooms. This came about because there was an area providing sheds for the benefit of the flats, but they were never used for that purpose and became neglected and quite filthy. Peter negotiated with the Council and we were able to take them over.

From what I can remember, our foyer was opened out as a wall was knocked down, and we had the underneath of the stairs of the flats in our foyer. I can't remember how this was all walled up but it evidently was. There was a yard between our building and the sheds, so we had to go out through the vestry, which we don't have now (due to later refurbishing) to the outside and into a door into the sheds. There was much work to do to get them into shape and I believe Clive Abbot was in charge of the operation. Bill Hill again with his DIY skills did much work out there and so did many others. There had to be lighting put in and decorating done apart from much cleaning.

Eventually we had accommodation for our Sunday School which we began to refer to as "Junior church". We had a few problems because of it being a separate building, one of which, it was quite cold out there. We did get some heaters which we thought were quite safe around children, but it was felt that the authorities wouldn't have agreed. However we managed for a while out there until a major refurbishment was accomplished and the sheds area is now incorporated into the small hall along with the walkway we'd had. God has always provided our needs, for which we are truly thankful.

Whilst Peter was with us there were changes between our three churches. Meadgate and St Paul's along with St. Mary's became a team ministry and Peter was no longer curate but a vicar, and then a larger Vicarage house was found for him. Peter was always interested in the ministry of healing and deliverance and, on occasions, he invited Bill or I to accompany him when he went to pray for people. He also gave us couples to take through a course to help them to discover a faith in Jesus.

A Church with a Building

Once Peter invited us to accompany him along with a few others to Bishop David Pytche's Church at Chorley Wood where we attended a service of healing. All these experiences have been very good because it has led us to study the Bible in a much deeper way and not only to read it but to *study* it. We have learnt so much of spiritual matters but know that there is much more for us and we are very excited in our faith.

Peter was with us for fifteen years and many of us are still in contact with him as we are with our previous curates. It seems that we never want to lose their friendship and fellowship.

After Peter and Diane left us to go to Westcliff-on-Sea, we were again in a period of interregnum. This time our two wardens were June Davidson and John Nightingale, so June with her knowledge and know-how led us through this period.

John and Anna Adams said "goodbye" to us at Easter 1980 amidst much sadness. Their time with us had been very profitable and they were very popular amongst the folk on Meadgate.

There followed a three month interregnum with Melvyn Sach acting as Vice Chairman of the Meadgate District Church Council (MDCC) which comprised of Clive Abbott, Mary Barton, Marion Bishop, Dorothy Bradley, Russell Cooper, Dot Cumming, Bill Hill, Tom Smith-Hughes and Melvyn Sach.

The Revd Peter Nicholson with his wife Diane, daughters Sarah (11) and Tracey (9) moved into the curate's house in Longfield Road on 18th June prior to taking up his appointment as Meadgate Priest in Charge in July.

Prior to this, 36-year old Peter had served four years as Curate at Christchurch, Croydon after training at Oak Hill College. Before his call to Holy Orders, Peter had served as an Avionics Engineer in the RAF working on Harrier Jump Jets.

Peter was a conservative evangelical with charismatic leanings. He had a heart for evangelism and saw the Meadgate Church as a challenge and the surrounding area as ripe for evangelistic endeavour.

During autumn of 1981 the curates' house had two new rooms added plus upstairs toilet and wash basin at a total cost of £6,900. It made for a much more suitable home for our new Curate and family.

It wasn't long before Peter had introduced Guest services and a week night meeting for children called Club 45 to which 100 plus would attend on Wednesdays at 6pm until 6.45pm, hence the name "Club 45".

A Church with a Building

Peter worked hard on confirmation classes and on 23rd November 1981 at St. Mary's Great Baddow, eight of our young people were confirmed. They were: Natalie Bell, Susan Bradley, Nicola Cook, Kathryn Davidson, Denise Passfield, Julie Richards, Michelle Tebbitt and Carl Williams.

During Peter's first year, he and the MDCC worked hard on revising and updating the Meadgate Church Constitution. At the AGM in March 1981 it was agreed to put the new constitution to the Parish PCC for ratification. Also agreed at the AGM was the establishment of a carpet fund targeted at £1,000 and the introduction of midnight Holy Communion on 24th December.

Year 1981 was a thriving year under Peter, with all the following activities going well: Sunday Services, Mums and Toddlers, Club 45, Playgroup, Wives Group, Senior Citizens group, Youth groups, Bible study and prayer groups.

10th January 1982 saw the retirement of our popular Parish Rector Canon the Revd Jack Kingham after 30 years in Great Baddow. Meadgate has every reason for being eternally grateful for Jack's support for our church. Without his vision and weight behind the Meadgate Project, this book would not have been written.

Peter, our Minister, worked with great enthusiasm and vision. His two elders, Bill Hill and Melvyn Sach retained their youthful looks for two reasons:- Melvyn drank malted milk every night and Bill never ever drank Church coffee.

On 12-13 June 1982 we celebrated the 10th Anniversary of the opening of the church centre. Our speaker for the weekend was Revd Michael Stedman who was our curate in 1972 when the building was opened. Michael looked just the same, he didn't seem to have aged at all.

On 7th September 1982 our new Parish Rector was installed, he was the the Revd Jim Spence and we were able to welcome him to St. Mary's at the invitation of their congregation.

For the second year running our curate Peter broke down in his car on holiday and had to call the RAC which apparently stands for "Rescue a clergyman! In September we started a Meadgate Men's fellowship to be held on the 4th Thursday of each month. It was an encouraging start with 19 attending.

On 28th November 1982, seven of our fellowship were confirmed at St. Mary's by the Bishop of Chelmsford. They were: Julie Brett, Myrna Day, Helen Flynn, Stephen Fox, Stan and Dorothy Gill and Kay Thomason.

A Church with a Building

In 1983 the church was growing in number and our Sunday morning congregation was dubbed as the "Sardine Saints". Seating everyone at our 10am service became a growing problem. Experiments were carried out to change the seating arrangement by focusing the congregation towards the west window where the mobile platform was placed. This seemed to help and the seating remained in this configuration for many years to come.

During 1983 the first regular Music group was formed to lead our morning service. This was led by Russ and Chris Cooper, a young couple full of talent and who were destined to play a huge role in the service of the church for many years, not only as music leaders but as children and youth leaders.

In the summer of 1983, negotiations took place with the Borough Council to acquire some redundant sheds adjoining the church centre. These were no longer being used by the tenants and we proposed a scheme for converting the sheds for Sunday school teaching and for storage purposes. Plans were drawn up and formally submitted.

1983 was a very busy year with the many encouraging signs of growth. The Parish Magazine for January 1984 commented on the previous year as follows:-

> "1983 has been a difficult year on Meadgate. We have suffered more than our fair share of illness, bereavement and diverse other problems. In this respect we wish to place on record the wonderful work of Peter Nicholson. Throughout the year he has served with complete dedication as leader, pastor, visitor, counsellor, encourager and much more. Perhaps most of all he has been a genuine friend of Christ, a friend who has not let us down."

1984 saw the introduction in May of Cell groups in six different homes. They met every fortnight and the theory is that the cells grow and then separate and create new groups. Participating members would engage in Bible study, prayer and informal fellowship, thus making each member feel cared for in an atmosphere of mutual care and support.

Eventually the six groups grew to more and the cell group scheme went on very profitably for many years. Incidentally the word "Cells" had a meaning:

>   Caring
>   Encouraging
>   Loved
>   Learning
>   Sharing
>   *Notice the central word is "Loved", the basis of our faith.*

A Church with a Building

At our AGM in March 1984 the following members were elected to the Meadgate Church Committee (MDCC):-

Clive Abbott, June Davidson, Roy Davidson, Stan Gill, Bill Hill, Melvyn Sach, Jill Smith Hughes, Brian Smith, Judith Whalley. (Peter chose his elders:- Bill Hill and Melvyn Sach.)

In the summer, Billy Graham and his team under the banner of "Mission England" came and crusades were held on various football pitches around the country. Our nearest venue was Ipswich. Several coaches went from Meadgate during the Mission. This church sent round invitations to people in the community offering them a free trip to this event which was held every evening for a week. Our fellowship members were well represented. A few of our members joined the choir and so had to attend every evening. It was a spectacular event and we had a few people respond whom we then had to follow up. It was at one of these evenings when Jeff Hill made the decision to serve God by faith and give up his secular job.

In September 1984, our church received official permission from the Council to convert the redundant sheds into classrooms and storage space. Also in September, we had a reunion with two of our former curates. The Revd Tony Bishop having completed his time in Nigeria and the Revd John Adams on leave from ECM Austria. Together with our then current minister the Revd Peter Nicholson it made for a unique occasion.

The work to convert the sheds next door began in the Autumn and much of the work was done by the church members who among them displayed a wonderful assortment of DIY skills, none more that one of our Elders Bill Hill who conceived the whole idea in the first place. He and Clive Abbott played a major role in drawing up the plans and subsequent DIY work.

By April of 1985, the church annexe was complete and the opening ceremony took place on 21st April with our Parish Rector the Revd Jim Spence officiating. Doris Hill ceremoniously cut the ribbon across the door entrance. The church annexe commonly became known as "The sheds" and was a real extension to God's Kingdom in more ways than one.

1985 was a year when the "Keep Sunday Special" was in full swing. Peter Nicholson threw his weight solidly behind the campaign and encouraged us to individually write to our MP and actively support the campaign in every way possible to keep our traditional Sunday as a special day. Peter was always active in supporting Christian values and encouraged his flock to do likewise.

A Church with a Building

The fruits of Peter's ministry continued to grow and was evidenced by 14 of our young people being confirmed at St. Mary's on 24th November 1985.

In July our two oldest members celebrated their 96th birthday. They were twins: Mrs Blake and Miss Thomas. At that time they were the oldest twins in the UK. Also in July we started a youth club which met fortnightly between 7.30pm and 9.30pm on Tuesdays. Games such as Table Tennis and Billiards were on offer together with facilities to listen to music and have an informal chat over light refreshments. It was simply a meeting place for the 13+ age group with Christian supervision in mutual trust and friendship.

Mission Chelmsford.

Evangelist Daniel Couzens held his meetings in a Marquee in Central Park between 13th-28th September 1986. This was supported by many churches in the Chelmsford area as well as ours. Peter Nicholson encouraged us to get involved. He had a heart for evangelism. Meadgate Church had 34 referrals from the mission out of a total of 750 enquiries during the whole fortnight.

At the end of 1986 our Elder Bill Hill relinquished his position and his replacement was Clive Abbott who was Vice chairman of the MDCC. At this time there were 130 members on our congregational register. Peter was still taking many people through the confirmation course and on 23rd November 1986, the following people were confirmed:-
  Allan Bell, Michael Betts, Kim Darling, Sarah Fricker, Peter Glover,
  Janet Nunn, Vivien Oakley, June Peppiart and Michael Fisher.

A Church with a Building

One of the highlights of 1987 was the participation in the May Fayre in Baddow Park. Our own Russ and Chris Cooper organised a procession, with song, dance and music based on Graham Kendrick's "Make Way". This made for a dazzling display before hundreds of people during which the Gospel was clearly presented. Smaller productions were later made in several churches in and around Chelmsford.

1987 Street Parade (*headed by the Cooper's trusty Morris Traveller towing a model of Lord Shaftesbury mounted on a trailer*) leaving Meadgate and heading for the Recreation Ground to take part in the Great Baddow May Fayre.

On 14th December 1987, we said a fond farewell to two of our earliest members John and Marion Bishop. They moved to Baddow in 1967 with their children Elizabeth and David, by way of St. Mary's; they discovered the emerging Meadgate Church being held in the school and homes. At that time Marion joined our team of Sunday School teachers and participated in the "Wives Group" in which she subsequently became chairman. Her work became almost legendary. In addition to this Marion served on the MDCC for twelve years. Her husband John was a good background influence. Gifted with mechanical and DIY skills, he was used fully by the church in these capacities including the ever-repeating cause of "saving curates' cars". His horticultural skills often were seen in church floral arrangements. Our loss at their departure to Heathfield in Sussex was certainly to the gain of the church down there.

A Church with a Building

1st March 1988 heralded a major change in the Parish of Great Baddow. Hitherto St. Mary's was the mother church who had founded the fledgling St. Paul's and Meadgate churches. The two sister churches had grown to such a size that each was to become District Parishes in their own right. Therefore instead of being under the wing of St. Mary's with Priests in charge, each would now be led by a Vicar with St. Mary's having a Rector. The parish of Baddow at large containing the three churches would be known as "Parish Team Ministry". St. Mary's would still have Parish Wardens whilst St. Paul's and Meadgate would have District Wardens. Our own Priest in Charge Peter Nicholson overnight took on the title of "Team Vicar". Meadgate's first District Wardens were Clive Abbott and Ken Horton. The formal inauguration ceremony took place on 1st May 1988 and was presided over by the Bishop of Bradwell.

To mark the change in the Parish, Rosemary Baxter wrote a poem in the April magazine.

What's in a Name?

There are strange goings on in our churches,
In Meadgate, St Mary's and St. Paul's.
The Clergy are changing their titles,
The thought of it really appals.

Our Jim will no longer be Vicar,
But "Rector" you must understand,
The curates of the other churches
Will now be called "Vicar" - how grand.

But don't let these changes alarm you
For after all what's in a name?
Whether Curate, or Rector or Vicar
Their faces will still be the same!

In September 1988, Peter Nicholson, now promoted to Vicar, was presiding over a very flourishing and growing church. For the record here is a list of activities and leaders in the children's and youth work at this time:

<u>Children's club (Tuesday evenings)</u>:- Sue Dring, June Peppiart, Margaret Day, Rebecca Nightingale.
<u>Climbers' (Sunday morning)</u>:- Gloria Hobbs, Hillary Toseland, Helen Clarke.

<u>Explorers(Sunday morning)</u>:- Christine Cooper, Sarah Dixon, Bob Ryall, Kirsty Hazel, Mark Alder, Lesley Bragg.

<u>Pathfinders (Sunday morning)</u>:- Alan Hobbs.

A Church with a Building

<u>Munch Bunch (Sunday evening)</u>:- Jeff Hill, Carol Sach, Rick Ridgwell.

<u>Youth Club (Tuesday evening)</u>:- Peter Wyatt, Jeff Hill, Peter Kirk, Rick Ridgwell, Mark Philips and Allan Bell.

<u>Hawkwell Discipleship Course.</u>

One of the first things Peter introduced after being Team Vicar, was a Discipleship Course for the church fellowship. This course was written and prepared by the Revd Tony Higton the then outspoken and controversial Vicar of Hawkwell. It was considered very charismatic, emphasising the work of the Holy Spirit, baptism of the Spirit, prophecy, healing, all member ministry and speaking in tongues. The charismatic movement was in full swing in the UK and its influence had been felt in Meadgate for many years.

Peter could be described as conservative, evangelical, and charismatic as indeed could many members of our church, but not all! Some were uneasy about it and for a time there was a bit of tension in the congregation. However some completed the course and somehow the tension dropped eventually. There was enough love among us to overcome our differences of belief. Love after all is stronger than death. It has to be said that the course was a blessing to many, and lots of our members became more vibrant and committed Christians. It was a learning curve for us from which we all learnt a great deal, and became more mature and tolerant people as a result.

Also in 1988, Jeff Hill was appointed Meadgate Evangelist. He was commissioned on 4th December.

Jeff trained for one year with British Youth for Christ, and gained valuable experience and training in schools work, street work and evangelism in Youth clubs and Coffee Bars etc., all of which he was able to put into effect on his return to Great Baddow and Chelmsford. He went on to Bible college where he met his lovely wife Julia and on completion of their time at college, they married and later entered into the Church Army. He is currently serving the Lord in Witney, Oxfordshire, and he and Julia have five children; not bad for the one we all thought was a confirmed bachelor.

A Church with a Building

Farewell to the Abbott family.

Sadly the time came when the Abbott family made the decision to move away. Since the opening of the church building on 18th June 1972 Clive and Janet were involved in numerous ways in the life and work of Meadgate Church. Clive served in various capacities including Deacon, MDCC member and Vice Chairman, Treasurer and Warden, and was often the preacher on Sunday mornings. Many will recall the Abbott/Sach productions of Family Services. Janet worked amongst children and young people including Playgroup, Munch Bunch and Pathfinders.

When Emily Burlington asked for Baptism by immersion, because she had not been previously baptised, Peter was happy to carry out this request and it took place in the swimming pool at Meadgate School on 16th June 1996. It was quite a special event. Some members of the Chelmsford Mission Choir joined us in our church service and then we made our way to the school swimming pool. Our music group led us in worship and words were given by Peter Nicholson and Ken Horton who went into the pool with Emily and both baptised her. Claire Dawkins was her sponsor. After this ceremony we were allowed to have a swim in the pool and mostly the children took advantage of this opportunity. This was a special occasion for Bill and myself as Emily is our precious granddaughter. We were so thrilled that she had grown up in our church and made the decision for herself that she wanted to be baptised. It was a baptism by immersion because she had only been dedicated as a child.

Emily Burlington being baptised in Meadgate School swimming pool.

A Church with a Building

Some years later we were to have the same thrill and delight as Alice, Emily's sister, made the same decision and as far as I can remember, she and about three others were the first to be baptised by immersion inside Meadgate church. A portable baptistery was borrowed and Revd Mones Farah baptised them.

Peter and Diane Nicholson stayed with Meadgate for sixteen years. They were years of growth in our church and a spirit of togetherness prevailed through thick and thin. As a church family much love permeated the atmosphere, but of course as with any other fellowship, there were disagreements and tensions at times. Not everyone agreed on all the finer points of Biblical doctrines or teaching. Of one thing we did not compromise on was our oneness in Jesus. This has never been negotiable in Meadgate Church. It's in Jesus alone that we trust and hold as the basis of unity. Our unity is solely founded on the person of Jesus Christ and His saving grace.

During his time at Meadgate Peter was our minister and friend. He showed good leadership qualities, sound biblical teaching, good pastoral care and all-round ministry. Peter was strong on administration, efficient and orderly in all he did. Diane his wife gave him steadfast support throughout the years they were here. Our fellowship became very attached to the Nicholson family, we saw their two daughters Sarah and Tracey grow up. It would seem strange without them but the time came when Peter felt called by God to move on. We realised that he had given his all to Meadgate and on 8th September 1996 moved to Westcliff-on-Sea to prepare for his role as Vicar of St. Michael's and All Angels.

In the meantime, the MDCC were looking at ways of enlarging our premises, but the realisation of this vision had to wait a few more years down the line. Again it was time to clean up the vicarage and decorate it.

The Second Vicar

A new Vicar was eventually appointed. It was the Revd Mones Farah and his wife Sally who were coming to take us on. They brought three children with them, the eldest Elizabeth, then Eleanor and little Mary-Anne. Mones and Sally were able to choose their wallpaper and whatever else we could do for them, our team of helpers set out to do. Ken Horton was our expert decorator, so he took on that task and since he was self-employed, he gave up a lot of his own jobs and made a wonderful job of the decorating. Some others of us did painting under Ken's guidance.

Whatever we did, we did it with joy and much laughter. We were happy that we now had a new vicar and we were into a new era and were wondering where we would be going from here.

A Church with a Building

Our son Jeff said we could expect a lot of good food and we have all since become aware of Mones' cooking skills.

Mones did make some changes. We had had our seating facing the west wall, and it was changed so that we were sitting front to back in the church with the Cross at the front(south). We also had the communion rail around the Cross and curtains surrounding the communion rail. We no longer had Family services, so the children no longer took part in the main service. We knew that we were going to be moving on to more adult style of worship and preaching.

We were still struggling with the Sunday School problem of not having enough room for our needs so it was decided to completely reorganise the whole building and to do so meant we couldn't meet there for a while.

Paul Brown took on the responsibility of the redesigning project. There was an arrangement with the Roman Catholic priest that we could borrow their building (a large hut at the top of Longmead Avenue, opposite the Fire Station which is now where the Doctor's surgery is) and we met there for many weeks for our services.

It was exciting to go down to Meadgate and watch the progress being made by the builders and we looked forward to our new building. It must have been a heavy load for Mones on top of looking after a congregation and services, not to mention his responsibilities as a husband and father. God always equips us, Praise His Name.

We were all delighted with the final results. We no longer had the sheds and the pathway between them and the church building. It was all incorporated into one. It means that the sheds area is now part of a second, smaller, hall, with two toilets at one end. The main toilets now adjacent to the Crèche room which are accessed through double doors at the back of the main hall and these doors open out into a cloakroom. To the right of the doors are the toilets with separate access to the Crèche room and to the left entrance to the new office. We were so pleased to be back in our own building. However there still seemed to be a lack of space for all the younger people to have their meetings. This was partly solved by the introduction of a cabin which fitted into the small yard just outside the main back doors.

As Mones leads the church on and more people are becoming members, I feel that in the future something will have to be done. God knows our every need and will supply as we put our trust in Him.

A Church with a Building

Mones and Sally have been exceedingly busy in introducing new paths in their ministry. They have travelled far and wide to learn new things of God and to bring them back to share with the congregation. This has led them to introduce soaking prayer, which is resting in God's presence along with worship and healing, first steps toddler group, parent café, Oasis café, intercessory prayer, and a prayer ministry team. Also an extra evening service mainly geared to younger people.

We now have a church staff team which comprises of a youth minister, youth team, office administrator, community worker and pastoral visitor. I think we are well taken care of under the ministry of Mones and Sally. Personally I am truly thankful for their care to Jenny (my daughter) and Jeff (my youngest son) and their families. Although they have moved on, yet still they often receive attention from Mones.

Bill and I are in our old age now and have spent fifty years of blessing being members of Meadgate Church. There are still things for us to do, but nothing like as exhausting as in the early days. We are so thankful to God that we can use our spiritual gifts, so we still feel part of the active life of our church. Our three children Peter, Jenny and Jeff have done their bit over the years and now that they have all three moved away to other parts of the country; they all say that they count Meadgate Church as their true Spiritual home and are always glad to attend services when they happen to be visiting us. Jenny's children also grew up in the church as Jenny and husband Jim were active members. Two of their children are still living in Chelmsford and Emily is still a member.

Sometimes during a service, I look around at the congregation and I feel a sense of awe realising what God has done and is still doing.

Over the years we have seen quite a few dear friends go to be with the Lord, but we know we shall see them again. Many of them came to know Jesus through the ministry of believers here, but we remember them with love and affection.

My hope and prayer is that Meadgate Church will always be thought of and remembered as :

"The House that God built."

Chapter 4
The Building

The plot of land offered by the council was on the corner of the service road which gave suppliers' vehicles access to the rear yards of the shops on Meadgate shopping parade.

Inspection of the plot. Canon Jack Kingham holds one end of the new building plans while Melvyn Sach holds the other, with other members of the Meadgate congregation.

The Building

The first phase

The new building, opened in 1972, consisted of one big hall, vestry, kitchen, toilets crèche room and an entrance lobby. On entering the lobby there was a space beneath a concrete staircase which was used by the tenants of the flats above. Outside the kitchen, in the lobby adjacent to the staircase was a large cupboard inside which were electrics (to do with the flats above the shops) next to which were the double doors to the exit to the yard at the back. Beside these double doors was a recess to the kitchen and in that recess was a small cupboard in which the Bibles and prayer books were kept. In the main hall between the kitchen and the vestry were two floor to ceiling cupboards which housed playgroup equipment. In the vestry was a cupboard in which were housed communion vessels and clergy robes etc., and an outside door. There was a large desk also in the vestry, so it was also used as an office. Sometimes we had Bible studies and other meetings in there.

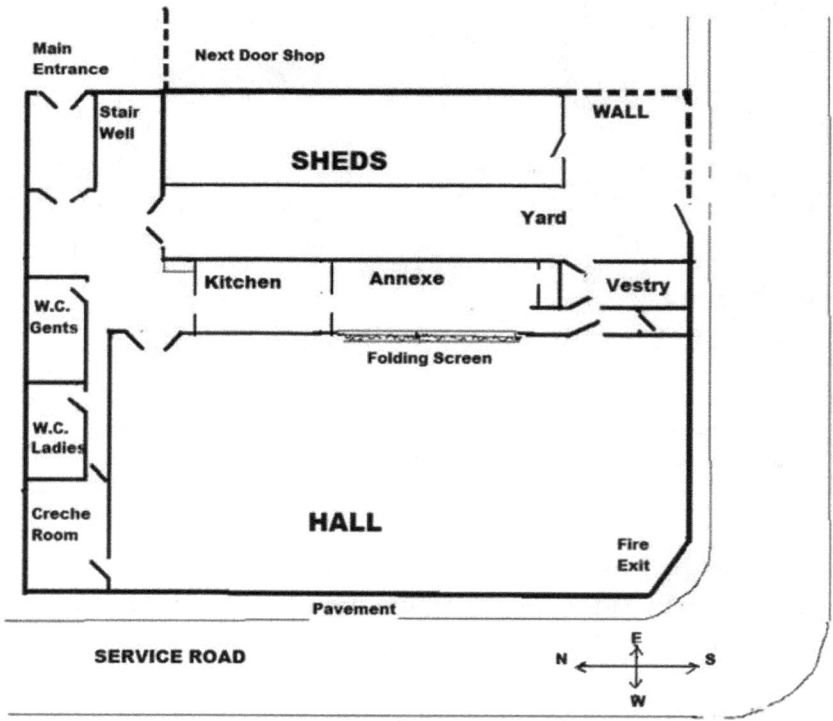

Phase I Layout

The Building

Sunday school had big problems because of lack of space but we managed to achieve some kind of privacy by screening off each group of children. These screens were made by Bill Hill and were used for many other purposes. The original windows were curtained. At the southern, cross end of the hall, there was the communion table, communion rail and the lectern and this area was closed when necessary by gold velvet curtains. Fire doors were at the southern end of the hall to the right of the Communion table. Fan heaters were fitted to the roof beams.

The second phase

The second phase (opened in 1985) consisted of acquiring, adapting and refurbishing the sheds across the yard (shown on the Phase I layout diagram) so as to provide accommodation for the Sunday School.

The rear of the church seen from the south. There were alterations in the third phase of expansion in which an emergency exit door was removed, although the outside step remains on the corner. The main entrance is behind the block of shops/flats.

The Building

The third phase

Further refurbishments and construction of a second hall were undertaken in 2001. The result of these changes to our original building, meant that the pathway outside the back of the building and the sheds (which had been converted into Sunday school rooms) are now part of the complete church, enabling us to have a larger kitchen, a small hall, though not that small, in which there are two toilets meant for the use of the children who would be using this hall for their Sunday school and a store room. There is also access to the kitchen from the second hall by a door and a serving hatch.

At the front entrance, there is a reception area in which the office is to be found. Leading in to the main hall there is a double entrance door which gives access to the main hall. At the entrance there is cupboard and shelf space on the left. Further into the hall on the right there is a door which leads to cloakroom space and the toilets and a back entrance to the office and to the crèche room. A further door at the other side of the main hall gives usual access to the crèche room.

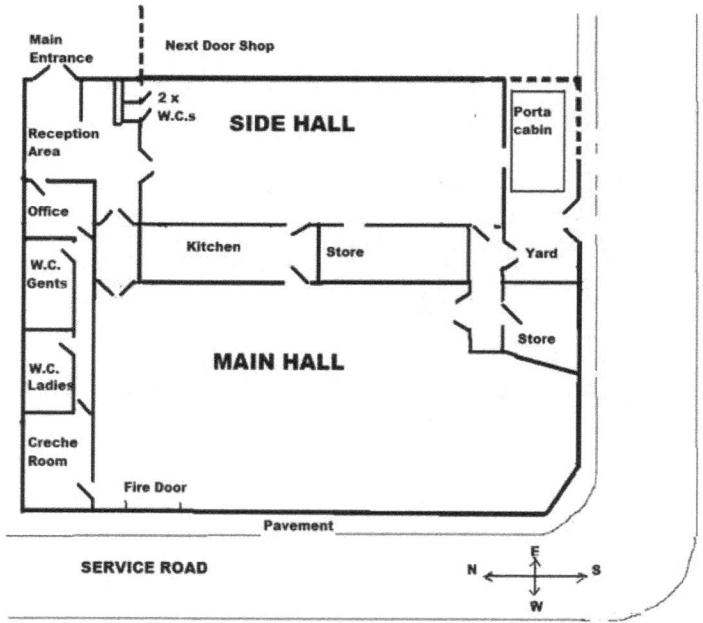

Phase III Layout

The Building

Just past the door of the crèche room, and coming to the outside wall there are double fire doors. The main hall has new windows more in keeping with a church building. The main hall kitchen hatch is almost halfway along the wall on the left and then the door leading into the kitchen. At the far end of the main hall there are double doors leading into a lobby and a double exit door. In this lobby is the door to a large store. Back in the main hall in the centre is the stage on which usually stands the pulpit, and this is where the musicians sit or stand during worship.

Portacabin

In 2005 a Portacabin was obtained and lowered by crane into the small yard at the rear of the smaller hall, mainly to be used as further accommodation for youth work. The location of this cabin is shown on the Phase III layout diagram.

Chapter 5
Progress of the Church

Numerical and physical growth

From its inception, Meadgate Church has changed from being a small Sunday School class in a private home, to being the thriving and lively church it is today. As the Sunday school grew in numbers, there was a need for the older children to meet elsewhere. An offer was accepted for the older children to meet in the home of a Doctor and her husband for the use of their home.

It was becoming known that there were Christians gradually being introduced to each other and various meetings were happening in peoples' homes as they got to know each other and share a vision for a church to be built. All this in spite of the fact that the Revd Jack Kingham already had this in mind. Meanwhile Terry Gilder applied to the Education department for permission to hire the hall in the local school. It too had recently been built. Permission was granted for this.

By this time our daughter Jenny had had sufficient piano lessons to be able to play for us at worship services which she did, at first in the school hall for our pre lessons worship, and also at family services. Then after Jean Sach joined our church, she also played piano. Grace Price has played for the services often and there are probably others but I just can't remember. Jenny has now moved away but was always happy to play when needed.

The Revd Michael Stedman came to the area as curate to St. Mary's Church with the intention that he would also take on overseeing what was happening in the Meadgate area. It was soon apparent that the Meadgate area was in need of his full time attention and so it was that he became the first curate at Meadgate.

Sunday school classes were now held in the school hall where the classes were divided up into the space available, but as the numbers of children attending increased, so did the number of teachers and soon there were too many for the hall, so other spaces had to be used where available. In the summertime on good days, classes were held in the playground. This meant tables and chairs were taken out and then put back where they were taken from.

Progress of the Church

Eventually the new church was built. After many sites were viewed and found impossible, mostly because of parking difficulties, the site behind the shopping area was settled on. We were invited to gather together for a photograph on the site. Soon after, building commenced.

On the Sunday of 18th June 1972 a service of dedication was observed attended by the Revd Neville Welch, Bishop of Bradwell along with the Deputy Mayor and his wife and other clergy. Melvyn Sach and Doris Hill were invited to do the readings.

1972. Service of Dedication for the new Meadgate Church building.

Subsequently there were to be further alterations and buildings to be planned.

Progress of the Church

During the time of Peter Nicholson's leadership, Bill Hill put forward the information that the storage sheds, which were Council property and were meant for the residents of the flats above the shops, were unused and it would be a good idea to approach the Council with a view to renting them for Sunday School classrooms. Peter Nicholson hadn't realised they were there and he was quite excited about the idea of obtaining them for our use. They were not being used for the purpose intended.

Peter approached the Council, who sent a surveyor and they found the condition they had fallen into and allowed them to be used by the church.

This meant much cleaning, painting and furnishing for us to do, plus wiring for electricity. There were no heaters in them, so we had to buy some. This was an anxiety for we had to consider the safety of the children. In the summertime there was no problem, so in the winter, Jim Burlington would go in early in the morning, put on the heaters and leave them until the children entered and then they were turned off. It seemed to work and was warm enough until lessons were over. There was another problem and that was that when the children went to their classes, they had to go out of the back vestry door across the path to enter what was once the cycle sheds. This was all right if the weather was dry, but getting across to the rooms was a stampede if it was raining. However we coped very well and very much appreciated having the rooms for each class. We even had a large area where we could have a time altogether where we sang choruses and had prayers etc.

After the departure of Peter Nicholson to take up the post as vicar to St. Michael's, Westcliff-on-Sea, we duly saw the arrival of Revd Mones Farah and his wife Sally with their three children Elizabeth, Eleanor and Mary-Ann.

It soon became evident to Mones that our building was too small and our committee began discussing the possibility of extending. Amongst our fellowship, we were blessed to have Paul Brown who is an Architectural Consultant and he set to work and the outcome is what we have at this time. I assume there had to be all kinds of legal requirements and building regulations etc., but finally we got the go-ahead to achieve what we have at this time. It meant that we had to have our services elsewhere whilst the building work was going on and we were lucky to be given permission by the Catholic Church to use their large wooden hut which was located where the Baddow surgery now stands.

Progress of the Church

When we eventually returned into our newly transformed building we arranged the layout according to revised building structure. Doreen Thompson made the magnificent tapestry (with a cross and a dove as its central feature) as the focal point of the big hall. In front of the cross is the stage on which a keyboard stands along with other equipment belonging to the Music group. This is where they gather to lead us in worship. Our pulpit also stands on this platform. This pulpit was donated in memory of the late Percy Walden by his wife and children. Bill Hill made a step to aid people to get up onto the stage. Young people are able to leap up easily, but the step is needed by many.

When this extension was being planned, it was decided that we should have new windows which would be more in keeping with a church than the previous ones. We were so happy to be back in our own building again and very happy with the new construction. Again Thanks be to God for his blessings to us.

Outreach

At Meadgate we have always been aware of our responsibility to be witnesses in our community and many events have occurred to this end.

During the period of Michael Stedman's curacy, there was a lot going on about which the local community were informed and the Sunday Services in the school were well attended by the not so often church-goer. At this time we had some people respond to the invitation to meet with Jesus, some now at this time are still members of our church.

We had, once a year, a Sunday School outing which took quite a lot of organising. Melvyn and Jean Sach were very good at this and we as leaders in charge of the children, were very anxious that nothing should go wrong, especially Jean and Melvyn. Some of the children were accompanied by a parent and in some cases both parents. Always a good time was had by all. We mostly went to Walton-on-the-Naze.

We were the first to hold a fete on the school playing field which was a huge success. By now we were well known for who we were and what we were there for. There was always a good atmosphere among us as a community. When the time came for Melvyn to step down from organising this event, Ken Horton took up the mantle and our young people had grown, some were adolescent, so it became more of a church annual outing. We had tug-of-war and the younger men would play football.

Progress of the Church

One of the 'tug-of-war' teams

At one of the venues, there was an opportunity for people to take out a canoe on the lake, and on this occasion Rick Ridgwell in his canoe turned right over which gave us all a fright. It was a relief to see him emerge from the water. He was wet but safe. Thank God. Our elderly folk enjoyed these outings immensely. They were a real family time and we all had great fun.

Our latest annual 'fun day' events have been held at the home of Godfrey and Diane Chasmer. They have a large estate and a swimming pool. We have the Sunday morning service there followed by a barbecue, then lots of opportunities to fellowship and use the swimming pool. There is a bouncy castle for the children. We are so grateful for the generosity of Godfrey and Diane. May God bless them.

Every year on Good Friday, we joined up at the Chelmsford end of Meadgate Avenue with St. Paul's and St. Mary's for the annual March for Jesus, so we could be seen as we walked together along the Baddow Road into Chelmsford. This march still takes place each year.

Christmastime we were out in the cold in the evening for Carol Singing around the area and sometimes people would come out of their doors to listen to us and we would hand them a card telling them of all the services over the Christmas period. Every household in the streets we visited received this card. Children were really helpful in posting them into the letterboxes. When we had completed we always received a hot drink, hot soup and some refreshment which was welcome when we were so cold. Sometimes we had this in church and sometimes a church member would offer to do it in their home. Pat and Olwyn Kerrison moved from Meadgate Avenue to Whitehouse Crescent where we had soup on the carol singing night.

Progress of the Church

Russ and Christine Cooper were always passionate about outreach and organised a few marches of witness done in a spectacular style with a large open back lorry decorated and very colourful and with a special theme. They were skilled in doing this kind of thing and it always involved much work. Many church members were recruited to help in the decorating and other ways and we were so happy to march for Jesus. One time we dressed up in Victorian costume and marched around Great Baddow. Our evangelist and his co-workers would hand out "Journey into Life" leaflets along the route, and sometimes they were asked questions which gave them opportunities to share about Jesus.

During Peter Nicholson's time as minister at Meadgate, there were several major outreach programmes associated with the Billy Graham evangelistic mission to the UK and a local diocesan programme of events called 'Mission Chelmsford'.

During Mones Farah's time as minister at Meadgate, there has been a broadening of the concept of mission with annual trips to Israel, often to help at the hospital in Nazareth, and various individual or small teams going out to Burundi, Albania in August 2013 to China. Within the UK there have been mission visits to places in Wales and frequent youth team attendance at Soul Survivor events.

At the time of writing, we have a team going out early on Sunday mornings to be a presence with people from other local churches at a car boot sale at Boreham. This is an outreach to people around the Chelmsford area not really to our community. However it is an outreach in the Name of Jesus and our team have had many opportunities to share the gospel and show their love and caring.

Since May 2011 Meadgate in cooperation with other local churches has been active in outreach at the Boreham car boot sale on Sunday mornings with its Church@CarBootSale van and coffee stall.

Chapter 6
Notable Events

Obtaining the Church Site

After viewing various sites, the Revd Jack Kingham and the Revd Michael Stedman must have almost given up hope of finding the right place for this much needed church to be built, but God had the right site in mind and it came through the Chelmsford Borough Council. They had identified a site for a Community Centre and decided to offer it for the building of our church. It was arranged that a group of us would stand on the site and have a picture of us reviewing the land on which we would have it built.

The site is not evident as seen from the shopping area so to this day it amazes people that there is a church there, in the corner of the shopping parade. There was a blank wall between two shops and under the flats above. To have a prominent entrance we were permitted to open up this wall and put in doors which is our main entrance into the church. This was a real blessing otherwise our main entrance would have been behind and out of sight so hardly anyone would have known there was a church behind the shops.

Meadgate Church entrance in the corner of Meadgate parade of shops.

Notable Events

Dedication of the building

When the building was eventually completed we had an opening and dedication service which was attended by our then Bishop of Bradwell the Rt Revd Neville Welch. Also present were the Revd Jack Kingham, our curate the Revd Michael Stedman, together with their wives and families, the Revd Peter Samson from Springfield Baptist Church, the Revd Mary Wyatt (Congregationalist) and the Revd William Mann (Methodist).

We were all set for being the Church of Ecumenical Experiment which we were designated to be.

First local mission

The first major event that we were involved in was a Parish mission. A team of students came from St. John's College, Nottingham under the leadership of the Revd John Goldingay. We had many home meetings and made lots of visits in the community. Our home visits were designed so that we could invite non-Christians to come and learn about Jesus. We had a few people whose lives were changed through the mission of these students and it was a time of great joy.

Outings

Right from the beginning, we were having Sunday school outings and these were always a wonderful time of togetherness. A day on the beach at Walton-on-the-Naze, playing games, having a picnic and generally having fun. We never ever lost a child which was a relief to Melvyn Sach. He took all the responsibility. Later this changed to being a Church outing because by this time we had mostly children from Christian parents in the Sunday School.

Nevertheless these were always enjoyable times. We knew how to have fun and it was amazing how many good footballers we had in our congregation. We had a team of players who had matches with other churches in the area and the results of the games were usually announced with the notices on Sunday. These matches continue to this day.

An inter-church football match

Notable Events

Christine and Russ Cooper, always amazing at organising events, planned to do a spectacular witness event in the Recreation Ground. Every year the May Fayre took place there.

Christine tells me that the idea came to them at Spring Harvest. Apparently Ishmael wrote songs and led the worship in such a way that it inspired them to reword some of the songs and turn it into showing how great it is to go God's way which is "Glory" and how sad it is to be a misery coping with the trials of life without Him. Thus the "Glories" and the "Miseries".

Russ and Darron Mead put the musical story together for the presentation of the gospel. In the story Tom Smith-Hughes, Lesley Ventham and Bob Ryall had an adventure and met the Glories and the Miseries. Tersha Bragg, Cheryl Mead and Clare Flynn led a top quality dance routine and Baddow got the message of the gospel

Christine decided that the Glories would be in bright yellow costumes and the Miseries would be all in black. This meant that lots of costumes had to be made, and Christine came to me with a large bale of yellow material and a pattern of how they were to be made and she organised how the miseries would be attired. Also she spread the news around Baddow that each church could be involved in this event and that sewing help was needed. Russ in the meantime was busy organising a cab and trailer which would be decorated in accordance with the march which would lead up to arriving at the ground. Russ also was responsible for the music side of it, as the Glories and Miseries would be dancing to the songs.

I set to make the first two or three Glory costumes and I managed to cut them out in sizes and before long people were phoning to ask if they could help with the sewing.

People from each church in Baddow became very enthusiastic in the event and it created a lot of excitement. There was a lot of preparation going on for a long time. Those who were Glories and Miseries were busy learning their dances, also the words of the songs and the sewing team were busy putting together the costumes. Others were making decorations for the float (the cab and trailer).

It really felt like we were doing a West End spectacular. It was a tremendous witness for the Lord, just what Russ and Christine were always passionate about.

Notable Events

1987 A scene from the Meadgate Church presentation of the 'Glory Story' at the Great Baddow May Fayre.

Glory Story was not the only event we did for Baddow. Again it was Christine and Russ who led us all in another event where we were all to dress in Victorian costume. This was to commemorate the life of four famous men who led by God made a huge contribution for good in the country. St. Mary's presented William Carey, St. Paul's CT Studd, URC William Booth and Meadgate presented Lord Ashley Cooper (a distant relative of Russ Cooper) known as Lord Shaftesbury.

Visit of the Bishop of Kitale

The Rt Revd Kewasis Nyorsok, Bishop of Kitale in Kenya made a visit to Meadgate Church on the 16th May 2004 and preached at the 10.30 am Sunday service explaining how he became a Christian as a young boy after meeting Philip and Grace Price, the first white people he had ever seen, when they came to his part of Kenya as missionaries in the 1950's.

After their retirement Canon Philip and Grace came to Meadgate to live in a house just a few hundred yards from the church, where they became regular attendees at services, at which Philip often preached and participated in many other church activities. (Philip was taken to be with the Lord in 2010.)

Notable Events

Visit of YWAM team from Argentina

In January 2006 a team of nine young people of various nationalities came over from the Youth With A Mission (YWAM) Discipleship Training School in Argentina and participated in youth outreach work based on Meadgate and St Paul's churches. At Meadgate they refurbished the newly installed youth-work Portacabin and at St Paul's helped with youth work project in a double-decker bus, as well as participating in local school assemblies.

Confirmations

Confirmations of members of Meadgate Church had usually taken place at services in St Mary's parish church, but on the 7th November 2010, the Bishop of Bradwell, the Right Revd Laurie Green confirmed eleven candidates at a well-attended service in Meadgate Church.

Visit of the Home Secretary

Home Secretary Rt Hon. Theresa May visited Meadgate on the 18th November 2010 and met with local leaders and residents in the main church hall to explain government policies and discuss any concerns about security and policing issues.

Meadgate Community Festivals

These festivals started in 2008, usually a summer festival and a Christmas festival in December. The festivals are for the local community and much of the activity takes place in and around the car park, which is cleared of cars for most of the day. For the organisation of these events the church coordinates with the local landlord (Chelmer Housing), the city council, the police and other local bodies.

The summer festivals usually offer performances by local dance or gymnastic groups in the car park area. The church side hall is generally used as a café area and an outdoor team of cooks provides free barbecued food. The December festival is usually followed by a service of Nine Lessons and Carols followed by mulled wine and mince pies and the music group generally provides an out-door 'rocking carols' performance.

Notable Events

Sunday 4th August 2013, the Revd Mones Farah (left) welcomes the Mayor of Chelmsford to the Meadgate Summer Festival.

Chapter 7
Features of the Meadgate Fellowship

Lay and ordained ministry

Although over the years overall leadership at Meadgate Church has been vested in a Church of England clergyman, right from the start it also had lay people very involved in various ministries: preaching, teaching and leading various activities and projects. This lay involvement has continued and under Mones Farah's time as minister has expanded, especially with young people taking on some of these roles.

During the period of Tony Bishop's curacy, he took on the task of training Lay Readers and quite a few people took advantage of his teaching. Thus it began to encourage others to offer themselves to preach at the services, which was a big help to Tony and to subsequent ministers. Apparently at the present time Meadgate has 21 lay people authorised by the Bishop of Chelmsford to preach and to lead our services. They and other lay people also lead and teach in house groups.

Visiting preachers and evangelists

Meadgate Church has long had a tradition of welcoming visiting preachers and teachers. Our first visiting preachers were theological students from St. John's College, Nottingham and they came under the title:- "Men for the Ministry". We were excited about their coming and made a display board for above the church doors. Unfortunately a mistake was made because the words read:- Men for the Ministry. We were quite embarrassed and had to change it. However it didn't take away the pleasure we had in welcoming them and hearing their plans for us during their stay.

We have had many visiting preachers over the years and we have had much teaching and we have learned much from their experiences. We were blessed at one time by the ministry of the Revd Clive Calver and his team who called themselves "In the Name of Jesus", and they came to bring awareness to us of the Charismatic teaching of healing and deliverance. This was all new to us and was a bit controversial at the time.

Graham Kendrick was among the team and he gave concerts in our Baddow Churches and at the Odeon cinema in Chelmsford, which has since been replaced by a bigger cinema with different performances.

Features of the Meadgate Fellowship

Bill and I were very privileged to have Graham stay with us for the two weeks they were here, and he ministered to us privately, sang with us and prayed with us. We were truly blessed. Graham was a famous hymn and song writer and was later very involved in organising the March for Jesus in London.

These marches happened for three years running and many from our church went on the marches carrying our Meadgate Banner and singing Graham's marching songs that he had written for the occasion. We were so excited and uplifted. The number of Christians who came on the march far exceeded the number predicted.

Marching for Jesus in the rain.

Getting back to the two weeks the above mentioned team were here in Great Baddow teaching us and ministering to us, we learned much about the wonderful things God was doing and many people here were healed and many delivered from demonic activity in their lives. I'm so pleased that I was able to experience the joy and expectation of great things happening here and elsewhere in the country. It spurred me on to learn more about Jesus and to get deeper into God's word, and to learn more about God's power over the enemy.

Features of the Meadgate Fellowship

There have been other well-known leaders who have been to Meadgate Church to share new things with us from God's word. John Leach and his wife Christine came for a weekend, John to teach about charismatic prayer and healing, whilst Christine mainly ministered in the children's work. Also they spent time in personal needs of our congregation and many of us were helped emotionally, spiritually and in our understanding of the Bible.

Bill and I were blessed to host another preacher named Derek Cook. If I remember correctly, he was from the Baptist denomination. Derek was musical and was a former dance band leader. He was involved in the Movement for World Evangelism and Maranatha Ministries. He gave us a record entitled "Inside Information" which has blessed us greatly and continues to do so.

J John has been to Great Baddow on two occasions. He is always good to listen to as he is so humorous but always gives us something to ponder on and we have greatly benefited from his teaching. One of the occasions he was here just for Meadgate Church but of course people from other fellowships were welcome to join us.

Inter-Church events

Over the years, we have had many inter-church events and the gifts that God has given us has always given us the opening to use them in the course of teaching, music, singing, acting and presenting. Whatever gift we have been given, we give thanks to God and give him all the glory. We can do nothing without Him, and have always tried to use them in his service. Some of us feel maybe that we don't have outstanding gifts, but whatever God's given us, I feel that we can make a difference to people's lives. Love is the greatest gift we can give to each other and I feel we do that in our church.

So many have put their gifts to full use and are really blessed and happy to have been part of God's work here.

We have in the past had lots of inter church events:- A sponsored 48-hour Bible reading which needed a church person to verify completion. All participants spent the night in the church, visitors included. Three groups rotated and completed the New Testament and then started on the old. Reading and working it out together was the aim. Chris and Russ Cooper were overseeing this event.

Many activities were organised which involved young people of all ages, with the hope that they would grow up believing in the Lord Jesus Christ, but leading and teaching them in a way that was exciting and enjoyable. To this end many able and willing church members worked extremely hard and gave so much time to it.

Features of the Meadgate Fellowship

Social events

Amongst all this we have had lots of secular events such as Barn dances, auctions. quiz nights and all-age fashion shows to which we have invited people from the community.

Once we had a performance of "Stars in their eyes" in which various people who had a talent for mimicking a famous stage performer did their imitation of him or her. It was amazing what talent emerged that night.

Mesdames Jill Smith-Hughes and Doris Hill modelling at a Meadgate fashion show.

For quite a few years we have had alternative to Halloween events which were always very successful and hopefully made people think Halloween was not a good thing according to Christian belief.

Also for a few years, Jeff Hill led a holiday club in the month of August and these were also appreciated by many in the community. These were discontinued on account of the lack of people available to organise and run this event after Jeff left to go to Bible College. However since the Revd Mones Farah came there have been regular trips to the Soul Survivor summer events and various other trips out.

Features of the Meadgate Fellowship

Another past event was the Tear Fund Hunger lunch which was organised by Rene Duke. This usually followed a service in which Jill and Tom Smith-Hughes (Reps for Tear Fund) would bring us up to date on news of how this fund was helping people in famine areas through people donating.

Many of our fellowship enjoyed the Spring Harvest events which happened every year around Easter. The first one of these was at Prestatyn and quite a lot of us went to this event. We learned so much, there were excellent speakers and there were ministries for all kinds of problems that Christians were experiencing and many were helped by prayer and laying on of hands. Bible study each morning was led by prominent Christian Bible Scholars, worship by well know Christian musicians. There were many seminars on different areas of the Christian life and it was hard to choose which one to attend. Spring Harvest was always hosted by Butlin's Holiday Camps. The first one was at Prestatyn but subsequently they have been at Minehead and Skegness. They are very popular and one has to book up early to get in.

Junior Church

On Sunday morning there are the various ages of Junior Church classes to learn about our Jesus, our faith and to have some fun activities. There is Crèche for 0-3 year olds, Sparklers for 3 ½-6 year olds,Transformers (now called Ignite) 7-11 year olds and The Furnace for ages 11-16 year olds.

Meadgate school use the church building for their Christmas and Harvest events and that gives Mones and his team opportunities to engage with the teachers and children.

Community events

We have always had it in mind that we are here for the community of Meadgate and have shown our love and caring in various ways; for instance we have had Christmas lunches for lonely people, which was sacrificial for the helpers as most have families and had to give up their day for this event.

We have had for several years community events outside the church with a barbecue in the shopping area, a bouncy castle, face painting and other events for the children and some stalls where people can display and sell their artistic wares. These are always popular. It's like a day out for the community and ways in which we can make new friends. The church is open and tea is always available.

Features of the Meadgate Fellowship

In the main hall we now have a large screen and on occasions there is a film showing and on special football events e.g., England v another team, the match will be shown and anyone can come to view it on the big screen. So there are lots of events in which non church people are welcome.

On the second Saturday of every month the Oasis Café is open in the side hall for breakfast right through to lunch and it is not just for church members. It has become quite popular and many people from the community call in during this event. Also there is a coffee shop open to all every Monday morning and this is an opportunity for leaders to meet with people who are shopping next door at the Co-op. Bill Rogers is nearly always outside to welcome them and invite them to come in for coffee and other refreshment. Often leaders have been able to listen to their problems (if any) and offer prayer. It's a morning when people meet with their friends to chat or if they are lonely, there is always one of the leaders to befriend them. It is very worthwhile.

Fun cooking lessons for every ability are offered at times and these are held at the church on a Saturday (as advertised) usually at 5.00pm at a cost of £2. This event comes under the title of "Two Fat Men".

Mones and his team get up early Sunday mornings in the summer season and go to the Boreham Car Boot Sale, where they have an opportunity to evangelise. They also serve tea and coffee and apparently the sellers and traders really appreciate them being there. We now have a van to transport all that they need with them to the site.

Soaking and prayer ministry

There is opportunity for members to meet with Sally Farah and her team for a time of waiting on God, Ministry and Prayer. It is called a time of "Soaking" and is offered before the Sunday morning service and usually an evening during the week. Many members find huge benefit from spending time just laying down in comfort and just meditating on the love of God. It is such a peaceful time of quiet worship.

The prayer ministry team meet before services to pray and hear any responses to prayer, which are given to the congregation near the end of the service with an invitation to come forward to be prayed for by the prayer ministry team. A large number of cards put up by individuals over a wide age range on the rear wall provide testimony of responses to prayer.

Courses

We always have in mind to obey the commission from Jesus to go out into the world and teach others about him so that all may receive salvation and a new life with sins forgiven. If we have love for others we will automatically be concerned for their souls.

Features of the Meadgate Fellowship

At Meadgate we are aware that there may be people on our estate wondering what Christianity is all about and that is why we have the Alpha Course. This course explains all there is to know about the Christian life and why it is so important for all people. After going through the course, people then have an opportunity to decide for themselves if they are going to receive the new life that Jesus offers and for which he gave his own life or walk away at least having been informed. The most important thing is that there is no pressure on anyone from any of us, but the hope of course is that the people who enter into this course will know Jesus for themselves and receive the gift of eternal life.

Up to now many Alpha courses have taken place and many new Christians have come to faith in Jesus Christ, which is always exciting. I always feel that we are rejoicing with the angels and so we are. At the beginning, Bill and I were participating in these courses, and always there was something new for us to learn for ourselves. Many other churches use the Alpha course and it is a really good way to explain what Christianity is all about. These sessions usually (but not always) take place in our church except for the away day and this is a time for the Holy Spirit as they learn about the outpouring of the Spirit at Pentecost, found in the book of Acts.

Mission support

Our church has always been keen to support Missionaries. Felicity Houghton, Anthony and Mollie Gregory, Steven and Joe Bishop and for a while John Adams when he left to minister by radio in Austria.

We have also supported others who have gone out from us to serve God in other fields, with, in 2013, teams of members going out to Israel, Albania and China.

Ex-members in Church work

We are quite proud of the fact that some of our younger people have left Meadgate to be ordained or to serve him in the Church Army, and these have received wonderful support from our church as well as from individual members. They all stay in touch and have a special affection for Meadgate church.

Peter Wyatt is now Vicar of St. Francis Church in South Croydon. Jeff Hill trained with the Church Army and is at this time serving in Witney, Oxfordshire. Mark Petitt is currently a curate serving two churches: St John's and St Mary's in Langdon Hills near Basildon, Essex. Gemma Stock was ordained in 2012 and is in her first curacy at Southend. Sandra Southee was ordained and is one of the Vicars based in St Mary's in this parish. We are all proud that they were at Meadgate Church and that they felt their callings whilst here. Occasionally they visit us for Sunday Worship and we are always overjoyed to share with them and their families.

Chapter 8
Music

In the early years when Sunday school began at 12 Marney Close, there weren't any instruments available and in any case no one who had musical abilities. It was at this point that I decided that my children should have piano lessons with the hope that we would have someone to play for us in our worship services. Jenny was the one who took up the task and she did well considering that she hadn't yet reached all her grades. Our first time with music came when Melvyn and Jean Sach joined the church and we were able to use the school hall in which there was a piano. Jean then began playing for us at the services, occasionally relieved by Dorothy Houghton, or one or the other of her daughters, Dr Josephine, and when home on furlough, Felicity (at that time was a missionary in Chile and later in Bolivia). Jenny Hill subsequently played for us on occasions. Our piano was donated to us in the beginning.

Our first music group was formed during the ministry of the Revd John Adams who was very gifted in music. He asked Russ Cooper to organise it and find the manpower and that was the introduction of guitars to our services. Bill Hill was also keen on playing the guitar and was more than willing to join Russ in the music group. Betty Mead joined as a singer along with others who have since left and moved on. Bill and Betty at this present time are still with the group.

1990's, Musicians of the 10.30 music group
led by Russ Cooper (left).

Music

Russ continued as leader for many years and since the start of the group, other guitarists have played for us including Peter Wyatt (now a vicar in Croydon), Peter Kirk, John Hom, Darron Mead, Steve Knights, Paul Brown and Andrew Brown. Some of them have had a time of leadership:- Russ Cooper, Bill Hill, Darron Mead, Steve Knights, Paul and Andrew Brown and Emma Smith. Singers:- Betty Mead, Sarah Dixon, Rosalind Coleridge, Duncan Mckenzie, these are on the regular rota, but often we see Emily Dixon, Luke Ridgwell, Pete Mckenzie and Nicolas Minnican. Others who have sang in the group in the past are :- John Nightingale, Bob Ryall, Janet Nunn, Allan Bell, Elizabeth Lloyd and Melvyn Sach. They have been very much appreciated for taking part in various events we have been involved in.

Currently the congregation are able to follow the words of the songs as they come up on a screen at the front. Anyone on the stage can see the words on a screen at the back of the hall. We have electronic equipment which is operated from a boxed-in enclosure at the back of the church and there is always someone there to operate the equipment and to sort out the amplification.

2013, Members of the music group at the Sunday 7.30 service.

Music

For the 5.30pm evening service it's currently mostly Jean Sach playing the piano for the hymn singing but occasionally when Jean is unable to be there, then Paul Brown will stand in for her. There is also a 7.30pm Youth service and for that the young people who are able to play an instrument will do so for their alternative rock style of informal worship.

Years ago, we would always go carol singing at Christmastime. Many times we had to brave the icy conditions, but were always welcomed as we knocked on doors and gave out invitations to services and the welcoming always warmed our hearts. We always ended up at someone's house for a cup of tea, mince pies and sometimes hot soup and rolls. It was decided that we should have a loud speaker for this purpose which would make a louder and more cheerful noise, so Bill set to work and made a trolley and he and Russ fixed it all up ready for use. John Kingham who is the organist at St. Mary's, made a recording of carols he played on the organ and that was very successful and made carol singing all the more meaningful. Sadly enthusiasm for this event dwindled and finally ended up with just two people turning up. That was the end of it and we haven't done it since. However for several years after that our carol singers performed in the Beehive public house. Currently, the 7.30pm service music group provide a performance outside the church under the title of 'Rocking Carols'.

We have much to thank God for regarding our worship and music.

Chapter 9
Artefacts and Memorabilia

In the early days of Meadgate Church, although we did not feel "poor" and were richly blessed, we belonged to a generation who had needed to be careful of resources, and were the original re-cyclers. There just wasn't the money or availability to spend money on things that could be made. We had lots of fun and enjoyed outings, parties and barn dances together though. These things stand out in my mind during the early days at Meadgate.

We had a moveable platform as a raised dais for the curate to stand on, which folded up when not in use. Our visual aids were inventive and interesting, with blackboards and easels, magnetic boards, felt boards and puppets. John Adams made good use of the overhead projector to illustrate talks and Bible readings. The hall was not carpeted then, but we used carpets which were rolled up when not in use.

The pulpit and furniture used for Holy Communion purposes were made of oak wood.

The communion table and one of several oak crosses positioned in the church halls.

Because we are a church of ecumenical experiment, we had trays with small glasses fitted which were used for communion sometimes and passed to each other.

Artefacts and Memorabilia

Originally a communion rail was used during Holy Communion services, but in the third phase of development the introduction of a raised stage area at the front made this impractical, so the rail was split into halves, each of which is mounted at the sides of the stage as shown above.

Holy Communion items: tray for bread, platter and individual glasses and two chalices.

Artefacts and Memorabilia

The Ministers' chairs.

I remember the kneelers which were used during Communion when we knelt at the alter rail. These kneelers were long boxes about 9" high covered in red fabric. They had many uses and were excellent seats for Pre-school children. I have fond memories of the "angels" sitting on them during Nativity plays at Christmastime.

A Christmas nativity play production, complete with 'angels'.
One of the red covered kneelers is seen lower right.

Artefacts and Memorabilia

We had a large oak wood cross where Doreen Thompson's quilted Cross now hangs on the south wall and a small cross on the window side.

People often donated objects in memory of loved ones, (clocks, Bibles and pictures etc.) A young Meadgate child named Rachel Abbott who had lost her sight due to a brain tumour, made a beautiful wall hanging of a cross, using latch-hook tapestry.

1970s Sunday school session. Note the wooden cross suspended on the wall at the back. The original piano is to the right of the emergency EXIT door right of the pulpit area.

In early years the music was usually provided by an upright piano, played by a number of people. I particularly remember Mrs Houghton (Felicity and Josephine's mother) who played with great enthusiasm.

Bill Hill made some very useful tables which folded flat and could be adjusted to two heights. These were used for many years, but seemed to get heavier with age !(maybe it was us ageing?) and some other folding tables were obtained for use in craft-work and for sit-down meals in the church.

Artefacts and Memorabilia

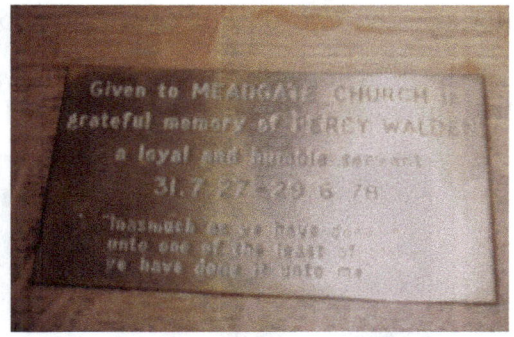

The oak pulpit was donated to Meadgate Church 'in grateful memory of Percy Walden, a loyal and humble servant 31/7/27 to 29/6/78' as recorded on a brass plaque with the quotation 'In as much as you have ye have done unto one of the least of mine so ye have done it unto me.' The pulpit is now fitted with a microphone.

At Christmastime we used to go carol singing around the estate. Bill made a trolley equipped with lights and sound which we trundled around the streets carol singing as we went. One year when it was foggy we lost Bill and the trolley for a while. This sound trolley was used for many other outdoor events throughout the year.

The sound trolley in the 1980s on a street march around the Meadgate and Longmead Estates (left) and at an event in Chelmsford (right).

Artefacts and Memorabilia

Our Lord has been so generous over the years and we now have unimagined comfort and modern day equipment to enhance our worship.

Most of the textual information above was donated to this book by Pat Davies and greatly appreciated by me Doris Hill, as I have greatly relied on her memories.

Christmas 2012. Members of the Music Group practice on the stage in the renovated main hall. Note the retained oak pulpit at the front of the stage and parts of the original oak communion rail at the sides. On the wall at the rear is the large quilted cross which is now a permanent feature of the church. On the side wall right is an area used for projection of song lyrics and liturgical texts. Front right is the oak communion table.

Artefacts and Memorabilia

Communications are given much importance in Meadgate Church and there has been substantial investment in equipment to upgrade and improve the quality of various means of communicating, whether with the congregations at the various services, the book and leaflet browsers, the visitors or the passers-by outside the front doors and large adjacent window.

Sound and vision control desk installed in an enclosure at the rear of the congregation seating area.

Shelving for Bibles, service books and hymn books at the entrance to the main hall, with letter racks for holding letters and leaflets addressed to individual members of the congregation.

Artefacts and Memorabilia

The library bookshelves in the entrance area.

Entrance area display to commemorate the fiftieth anniversary of Meadgate Church.

Artefacts and Memorabilia

In the 1980's many ephemeral artefacts were made by teams of adults and children for the various events associated with street marches and indoor events, often based on Graham Kendrick's 'Make Way' themes and associated worship songs. Above left: a decorated trailer that was towed in street processions. Above right: one of a number of decorated hoops carried in processions or used in dances. Lower left: a wall-mounted display. Lower right: a banner.

Artefacts and Memorabilia

Programmable video screen in the church entrance area and visible through the front window to people outside the church.

Artefacts and Memorabilia

Over the years Meadgate Church has been blessed with a succession of highly capable flower arrangers who usually make displays around the main hall for the Sunday services and other events.

A typical Sunday flower arrangement with the quilted cross wall-hanging featured behind.

Chapter 10
Publications

New Life

Even before Meadgate Church had a building, it began to contribute to the Parish magazine (called New Life) along with St Mary's and St Paul's churches, usually about one third each. This was a 12-page A4 publication and included announcements, marriage notices, reports of events, news items and drawings.

Baddow Life

From 2003 to 2012 a well-produced quarterly newspaper called Baddow Life was distributed free throughout the parish area, again with contributions from the three Anglican churches and Great Baddow United Reform Church. All 32 issues of this publication are available on the Internet at www.baddowlife.org.uk. For details of how Baddow Life was set up and organised, refer to Mrs June Davidson's account at the end of this chapter.

Reach Out

A church information publication produced in 1980.

Live Wire

In the 1990's Meadgate Youth Club produced an A4 size bi-monthly magazine called LIVE WIRE with eight to ten pages containing pictures, cartoons, stories and information of interest to the club members.

Study and worship publications

A four-page (A5 size) service sheet is currently produced for Sunday services (older pre-computer versions were on a single A4 sheet, printed both sides). The content has varied somewhat over the years but currently (2013) contains:

(1) a table of what services are available that day and who is leading, currently (2013) that would generally be **Pre-service**: 9.15am Soaking, 9.45am Prayer and sound check. **10. 30am Family Worship** or **Family Communion**, listing names of Leader, Preacher and Worship Leader. **5.30pm evening Service**, listing names of Leader and Preacher. **7.30pm Theme of service** (a celebratory type service with rock-style music group) listing names of Leader and Preacher.

2) 'Good News!' Short testimony statements, usually answers to prayer.

(3) Advertisement for coming event.

Publications

(4) Brief order of service for the 10.30 service. Any liturgical information and words of hymns are provided on a screen or can be read from printed service books

(5) Information on services for the following Sunday.

(6) Youth Church information (groups, ages and locations) for the 10.30am service. Currently Crèche (0 to 3 year olds), Sparklers (3½ to 6 year olds), Transformers, or Ignite since April 2013, (7 to 11 year olds), The Furnace (11 to 16 year olds).

(7) Member Notices and Announcements.

(8) Discover What You're Missing, lists all regular activities of church groups throughout the week.

(9) The Meadgate Church Team, lists church workers, functions and how to contact.

Cook Book

Michelle Wyatt produced a book called 'Meadgate Cooking', which was sold in aid of the church development fund with many tasty recipes contributed by church members.

Prayer course

For Lent 2013, Stuart Saddler of Meadgate Church had the idea of producing a 40-day prayer course titled 'Time to Pray', which was compiled by teams from the three Anglican churches in Great Baddow parish and distributed free in booklet form.

Vicar's Shout

This is a quarterly 4-page hand-out introduced by the Revd Mones Farah, which includes a letter and teaching from the vicar, news items and a list of future events.

Library material

Various information leaflets and booklets are placed on tables or racks at the entrance area and there are bookshelves stocked with donated publications on Christian topics which may be borrowed by members. Wallboards in the entrance area are used to display various notices and advertisements for activities and events, also for inspirational displays.

Bibles, hymn books and Order of Service Booklets

These publications are available to those attending services from shelves situated just before the entrance to the main hall.

Publications

Internet publications

Thanks to several members of the congregation having computer programming capability Meadgate Church website has been developed over several years and most information on the church activities and various downloads are available on the church website: www.*meadgatechurch.org.uk*

Baddow Life Newspaper - 2003 -2012

June Davidson on behalf of the Team representing three Churches.
When the Revd Mones Farah came to Meadgate Church as Team Vicar, he had many ideas. One was to have a quarterly Newspaper to be delivered to every house in the Parish. In 2003 a small group met at the Meadgate Vicarage to discuss the viability of such a venture. The idea being that it should be an evangelistic tool, have news of the three churches in Great Baddow, but also to include interesting news of the village including an information page, but we wanted it to be free!

After enquiries this small team went to visit the Weekly News Manager. We were made very welcome and from these small beginnings came an excellent newspaper.

We were given the costing's, which we envisaged would be possible to be met between the three churches, the paper would be printed and distributed with the free paper the Weekly News - at a week of our choice. We decided to centre the distribution on Christmas, Easter and Harvest, later agreeing a June issue.

On the team, which was chaired by Mones, we had sufficient gifts to produce the contents and a file of the newspaper was sent to the Printers for distribution in good time each quarter. We had a very good relationship with both the Printers and Distribution Department.

The first newspaper was printed in Autumn 2003 and 7,000 were produced, approximately 6,000 of which were distributed with the Weekly News and 1,000 by volunteers enabling every house in the Parish to receive a copy.

We started with one sheet (4 pages) but soon increased to 2 sheets (8 pages). Soon we developed advertising to help with the cost and also to give a service to local companies. Over the years we were almost self-sufficient, but advertisers came and went, but we were really pleased that so many stayed with us despite the financial problems at the time.

Publications

The small team met regularly under the Chairmanship of Mones and were very committed to the success of the paper. We would endeavour to keep up to date with Community news, and from the churches there were Testimonies, up to date news of Alpha, reports from the local Schools and up to date news of the Youth work from all three churches. Other popular features were the Restaurant Review, Crossword and Cartoon. So many people contributed and gave us interesting articles, and our Photographer took some wonderful photographs.

Sadly in 2012 we issued our last paper. This coincided with the Queen's Jubilee and the London Olympics. There was so much news we had an extra sheet to our farewell issue. A popular paper was now no more, but I think all things have a season and the Baddow Life had a long run, which hopefully was enjoyed by many, and helped them know that the Church is alive and well and ready to welcome all in to meet the Lord at any time.

Chapter 11
Testimonies

Early Days

By Rita Evans, wife of David Evans curate to St. Mary's Church at the time of the beginning of the first Sunday School at Meadgate.

We moved to Baddow in the summer of 1965 (I think). The Parish had just bought the house in Longfield Road to be a clergy presence on the Meadgate estate. I remember the house as being very small for its purpose. David could only just squeeze into his study. I think after us a study was built in the garden. We went on to use our home a great deal in our Ministry. Our first and second daughters Sarah and Kate were born in the house with the help of a lovely German/Lutheran midwife named Mrs Ford. Sarah in November 1965 and Kate in January 1968 in the snow. David was preaching on "The Fall" that Sunday and was on crutches after a tumble in the garden.

I spent much time walking through Meadgate with the pram en route to Chelmsford/Sainsbury and my doctor Robin Catlin in Baddow Road.

Whilst being very impressed and appreciative of the work yourselves, the Gilders and others were doing, this was David's first parish after being ordained and the next step in his training. Men had two parishes as curates before taking the responsibility of a living of their own. His time was spent with Jack Kingham at St. Mary's, being very involved with the Youth work in particular. I have more memories of that especially camping holidays we organised. He climbed the spire when it was being renovated (with the help of scaffolding I hasten to say), and he ran a Judo club with help,

So I guess ours were almost pre-evangelistic days in Longfield Rd. We moved on from Baddow to Walthamstow, a very different place and were thrilled to hear how the work at Meadgate blossomed. A story well worth telling.

Doris Hill comments.

David Evans was given responsibilities for the work that was being carried out on the Meadgate estate. He came once a month to the house to lead the Sunday School and to liaise with Terry Gilder about our progress. I remember him with affection for his interest and his caring for the children as well as his own input.

Testimonies

Sunday school starts

Terry and Beryl Gilders' account of how God led them to be at Meadgate.

Terry and Beryl were house hunting in Great Baddow. Both were teachers due to be married in August 1963 and had decided that Chelmsford would be a good place to live. Terry's vicar had advised that there was a lively parish in Baddow, so Beryl took the train to Chelmsford, visited a few estate agents and boarded a bus to Great Baddow. Having been given descriptions of only three houses in their price range, she was not sure where to start. Each house was in a different area of the village. She went into the church hoping for inspiration and warmth.

A large gentleman, wearing a dog collar approached. He introduced himself as Jack Kingham, vicar of the parish; and he seemed genuinely delighted to offer help. He looked at the house details and dismissed one immediately. Apparently a young couple would not want to live there. He felt that out of the other two possible, the Meadgate estate should be viewed first. The Meadgate estate had people and houses and nothing else. Doris Hill lived there and she wanted to start a Sunday School but needed helpers.

The next Saturday the couple made their way to the house with shutters, 507 Meadgate Avenue and viewed it. The price was right, it seemed to be in the right place and so it became their first home. Jack Kingham quickly introduced them to Doris who lived in Marney Close and the Sunday School was born. Doris had the vision, Beryl and Terry had the expertise and Jack was the facilitator.

Jack was good at finding jobs for people in his parish but having hundreds of houses in a short space of time with a parish church a long walk away was quite daunting. It troubled the curate, Stephen Taylor too. He did a lot of knocking on doors introducing the newcomers to the parish and telling them about the Sunday School. Norma Monck, who also lived in Meadgate volunteered to be a teacher, and she too did a lot of knocking on doors. Only two children attended the first session which was in Norma's house as Doris' father was living with them, sadly dying of cancer at the time. After his death, Doris was then ready to have school in her house as originally planned.

The Sunday School grew rapidly. The record was broken regularly, quite literally every time the number of children increased we smashed an old 78 gramophone record to celebrate. (they would be collectors' items now.) Two years after the start 30 children were attending regularly. Each session started in the hall and on the stairs with a hymn and choruses. Doris had the youngest in the kitchen, Beryl had the next group in the sitting room and Terry took the oldest group in one of the bedrooms.

Testimonies

Doris had parents knocking on her door, checking whether her home was a suitable place for their offspring. It was obvious there was a need for family services too. Some parents were asking for adult services.

The Meadgate church was beginning. We were outgrowing Doris' home. Jack Kingham went to the Bishop who declared that Meadgate could be designated "An area of ecumenical experiment". A house was purchased in Longfield Road and David Evans became the first curate to live on the estate. Adult services were held in people's houses but space was always limited.

Reg Spalding (who previously owned all the land that the Meadgate estate was built on and was still farming some of the land down to the river) offered a site and one of the first ideas was to build a large hall. Planning permission was not forthcoming. Another site, near the Chelmsford end of the estate was available but there were problems. David Evans moved on and in 1968 Michael Stedman became the new curate.

The school had been built by this time and the headmaster gave permission for it to be used on Sunday mornings for services. It became filled to overflowing with families. There were at least 5 classes which went out of the main service for instruction in classrooms whilst the adults listened to a sermon. We had family services too, when everyone stayed together enjoying a simple illustrated talk. The Church was growing into a sizeable community and everyone wanted a purpose built community church.

Our arrival at Meadgate
Michael and Gill Stedman - Our second curacy.

Our three years in Lindfield, West Sussex were due to come to an end in the Autumn of 1968 and in the summer of that year the Revd. John Sheldon, the vicar was looking for a suitable parish to which we could go. At a clergy conference he happened to meet Jack Kingham who was looking for a replacement for his curate, David Evans. They decided to do a bit of match making! As a result on the 24th September 1968 we moved from Lindfield to Longfield Road, Great Baddow.

A number of factors encouraged us to make the move. We were drawn by the enthusiasm and warmth of Jack and Nancy Kingham. Then there was the commitment of a small group of people who had been inspired by a vision and encouraged by Jack Kingham to provide a Sunday School to serve the families of the Meadgate Estate. I felt some excitement at the prospect of building something new on the foundation laid by David Evans. And finally, there were family considerations. Great Baddow brought us closer to Gill's family in Leigh-on-Sea and to my Mother who lived in Colchester and had recently been widowed.

Testimonies

The one negative factor was the house. We already had Simon, aged two and we hoped he would not be without a sibling. Frequently a clergy house has to serve not only as a home but also a place of work and of Church meetings. 55 Longfield Road was depressingly small. Fortunately the congregation of All Saints Lindfield had sent us off with a generous gift and in a moment of inspiration, Gill proposed that we used it to buy a cedar wood chalet. This we placed at the bottom of the garden to serve as an office. On Monday 7th October 1968 we were ready to start.

Priorities

My appointment was as curate to the parish church, but with additional responsibility to forward the work already taking place on the Meadgate estate. It was not long before it became apparent that these two tasks did not sit happily together. The demands of the Parish Church, particularly leadership of the work/among young people, made it difficult to give sufficient time to the developments which were taking place on Meadgate. A Sunday School had been launched in November 1963 with two children meeting in a home. This soon grew to the point when in 1966 it was necessary to meet in two homes.

The splitting of the Sunday School was very unsatisfactory, so it was a great encouragement when the head teacher of the Meadgate Junior School gave permission for the Sunday School to move into the Junior School on April 23rd 1967. This gave room to expand and enjoy more lively meetings. From then on the Sunday School grew rapidly increasing its roll to between 100 and 140 children and young people. From the Sunday School further developments took place.

A Family Service was held in the school hall on the last Sunday of every month, a wives group was formed, and informal meetings for older folk. It soon became clear that this growing Church needed a building in which to meet for worship, activities and as a centre for service to the people of the estate.

In 1965 David Evans had high hopes of being able to find a suitable site on which to build a church, but the various sites which were looked at proved unsatisfactory.

The building of the Church Centre

In the Spring of 1969 a site was identified behind the shopping parade at the heart of the estate. Negotiations took place with the Town Clerk of Chelmsford Borough Council who had already identified the site as one for a Community Centre. By the summer of that year agreement had been reached between the parish, the diocese of Chelmsford and the Chelmsford Borough Council for a Church Centre to be built.

Testimonies

The Borough council would lease the site at a pepper-corn rent, the Diocese would advance a substantial loan, and the Parish would raise the remaining funds to build and furnish the Church. There followed a lengthy period of preparation; the appointment of an architect and building surveyor and fund raising. Tons of scrap paper were collected and sold! During this period the Church community continued to grow; particularly among children, young people and young wives. The Meadgate Committee gave a great deal of attention not only to the raising of money, but also to the shape and style of worship which would be appropriate for a Church which would seek to be ecumenical and inclusive.

On the 28th May 1971 a report was given to the Parochial Church Council that the proposed Meadgate Church Centre was going out to tender, and on Sunday 10th October a photograph was taken of the Reverends Jack Kingham, Michael Stedman, and members of the Meadgate Committee on the site behind the shops.

On the 16th October a Memorandum was sent to the Bishop of Chelmsford detailing the origin and development of the Church Community on the Meadgate estate, and an outline of the vision for the future. On Sunday 24th October there was a brief ceremony marking the cutting of the turf in preparation for digging the foundations of the new Church Centre. On the 4th November a meeting took place with the Bishop of Bradwell when the dedication of the Church was discussed. He expressed his excitement over the project, and in particular that the Church should be recognised as an ecumenical fellowship under the wing of the Chelmsford diocese. He was cautiously supportive of the proposal to establish a team of lay deacons, appointed by the parish to share the leadership of the Church with the clergy.

In the same month of October a committee was formed under the leadership of Terry and Beryl Gilder to plan a Reception in the Junior school on 2nd February 1972 when a presentation of the project to the residents of Meadgate would be made, with an invitation to subscribe towards the building fund.

The opening and Dedication of the Meadgate Church Centre

Meadgate Church Centre was packed with an excited congregation for the dedication of the building (the thermo-plastic tile flooring not having yet been laid) by the Revd Neville Welch, Bishop of Bradwell at 3.00pm on Sunday 18th June 1972. The Rector, Jack Kingham and the curate Michael Stedman were present together with their wives and families and members of the Meadgate Committee. Also present were leaders of other denominations: The Revd. Peter Sampson (Baptist) the Revd. Mary Wyatt (Congregationalist), Pastor Anthony (Elim Pentecostal Church) and Revd. William Mann (Methodist).

Testimonies

Parish Mission

Between 16th and 24th September 1972, a parish mission was led by a team of students from St. John's College, Nottingham under the leadership of Revd. John Goldingay. The lives of many were touched by the love of God and several were profoundly changed. In a way this set the course for the Church to be a centre of worship, evangelism and pastoral care for the whole Meadgate community.

The Meadgate District Church

During 1972 and the beginning of the following year, a legal committee drawn from the three churches, St. Mary's, St. Paul's and Meadgate, drew up a constitution which made provision for three autonomous District Churches under the authority of a single Parochial Church Council. This gave considerable freedom for each church to develop its life in a way consistent with its particular context. With this in mind, a great deal of discussion took place on the Meadgate committee as to how our worship should express our ecumenical vision. The decision was made that when Holy Communion, or The Lord's Supper was to be celebrated, the service should alternate between the Anglican and Free Church styles. When in the Anglican form, robes would be worn and the bread and wine administered with paten and chalice. With the Free Church form, no robes would be worn and the wine administered with individual glasses. When the services were non- Eucharistic, no robes would be worn.

Some church members from an Anglican background felt that the church lacked the sense of a sacred space and of course, during the week the building became a Community Centre. But generally speaking the experiment was accepted, and indeed welcomed. During this period we were becoming aware that the time had come for us to pass the ministry into the hands of fresh leadership. We moved from 55 Longfield Road to Bergh Apton in Norfolk on Wednesday 15th April 1973.

A reflection on the Meadgate Experience
(Gill Stedman)

Looking back to this time, I have always thought that it was a good thing that the actual building work was delayed because it meant that the "church community" had time to grow together and become a reality before we had to deal with bricks and mortar! The frustrations, disappointments and delays over the building were many. Masses of time spent in meetings, planning etc. There were a lot of ups and downs, people threatening to leave and lots of oil on troubled water and diplomacy and some heartbreaks. But life is so often like that.

Testimonies

Leading the Woman's Fellowship was a lot of fun as a wonderful group of ladies grew to know each other better, through meetings, Bible study, outings and meals together. It was also at times a struggle! A memorable meeting was when someone was showing us slides of Oberammergau and about halfway through, I realised Timothy was on the way and sitting the rest of the evening on a hard school chair was very uncomfortable. I remember clearly the first meeting in the new Church centre and how different it felt from meeting in the large hall of the Junior school, (for which we had been very grateful). There was a real sense that somehow we were in a special place set apart for God's work.

Michael has mentioned the difficulties that our house presented and I don't want to go on about that, but it put us under pressure because of the conflicting needs of family with small children and providing a place for meetings. I did become an expert furniture mover - as did others in the church family!

I think that one of the most important aspects of the experience on Meadgate was the real and deep friendships that developed and that have lasted down the years. We shall always be truly thankful to God for those friendships and for the example that was given by others of commitment and service. When I was preparing this, I made a long list of names of all those special people that I can remember and each one is treasured. There was a real joy and excitement when people came to faith and as they grew in faith and commitment to Jesus. It was a time of experiment, pioneering, seeing what would work and what didn't. We were in many ways freed from tradition or what had always been done and although that can be at times rather scary, it was also a privilege.

We learnt some important lessons on Meadgate that have stood us in good stead through the years in other parishes. The way God drew people in to share in the church there, His faithfulness to us in times of darkness and disappointment, illness and tiredness. His work in our and others lives, His presence and goodness, His gifts of joy, fun and laughter. What a good word with which to end!

Our Memories of Meadgate Church
The story of Pat and Eddie Davies.

When we married and came to live in Longfield Road in 1966, the house opposite to us was owned by the Church and occupied by the the Revd David Evans and his wife Rita. Canon Kingham who was the Vicar of St. Mary's Church, had appointed David as a curate with a view to planting a new Church on the Meadgate estate. Longmead Avenue was still being built and the bridge did not exist, but with so many new houses and many young families there was a great need in the community.

Testimonies

However, although our Lord was building a Church among his people, a building did not materialize during David's curacy. We do remember the first ever Meadgate Church fete taking place on the school playing fields. It rained and David used our empty garage to dry the tents. When our son was born, David and Rita encouraged us to attend St Mary's Church where we were very happy.

When the Reverend Michael Stedman and his wife Gill were appointed, Michael was able to oversee the building of Meadgate Church on its present site. During this time we felt our spiritual home was amongst the emerging Meadgate Church. It was a very happy and exciting time.

The monthly family services took place in the school hall. We have fond memories of many dear Christian people who are now either with the Lord, or have moved to other parts of the country, but who have contributed greatly to building the Christian fellowship at Meadgate. We remember a very young man called Melvyn and his brother playing a guitar while singing choruses during the family services. Very innovative in those far off days.

A young wives group met at the school a few times. We really were young in those days, but now we have grown up and become CAMEO (Come and meet each other).

Michael was helping us to grow spiritually and took a group of us on a very foggy night to be confirmed at Heybridge, as we did not want to wait until the Bishop came to Great Baddow. This meant we were able to take our first communion on Maundy Thursday in the common room at Tusser Court. We had to sit on tables as all the chairs were occupied, but it was very meaningful to us and Maundy Thursday has always been special for us.

When the building was completed it was really good and God's presence was very real and tangible. Michael encouraged us to knock on doors and invite people to church and discussion groups, (some of the first house groups). This led to very real growth among many of us, but I do remember one gentleman who was hard to convince that Jesus did not come from a planet in outer space.

We had a mission in the parish when a group of people from a visiting theological college came and encouraged many of us to make a deeper commitment to Jesus.

We have a wonderful memory of an eight o'clock communion when the birds were singing outside and we were inside singing "Morning has broken like the first morning". Our Lord was moving in a special way and drawing many of his people to a knowledge of Him. Our children Mark and Susan were too young to attend Sunday School at this time, but that is another story. Michael and Gill were very special to us at this time as we shared so much joy with them.

Testimonies

We have always had much to praise and thank God for at Meadgate and He has always met our needs of the time with many special leaders and people. It is a great joy to see so many Meadgate children now taking leadership roles in the Church, and to see God working his purpose out with us during so many years at Meadgate.

The church has been an important part of our lives in Great Baddow, and truly enriched our married life with fun and fellowship. (We'll forget the hard work, it's now someone else's turn for that.)

We look forward to the future and praise our Lord for all the special people who have been and are now, part of Meadgate Church. We anticipate great things to come as the spiritual need seems greater than ever.

Eddie Davies

Eddie was inspired to write this poem for us during a Bible Study afternoon in his house and he had retired to his upstairs office:

MEADGATE CHURCH

In nineteen hundred and sixty three
When Meadgate was new and churches were few,
To the vicar of Baddow a request was sent
"May it please you sir, to support a new school
Where children may come to learn of God's rule"
The vicar replied with his gracious assent,
So in a home on the Meadgate, midst the shops and the flats,
The first pupils learnt what God's love meant.
And whilst at first its numbers were few,
With the passage of time the Sunday school grew.
And after some time the Lord said "Enough".
"You need a building new, where the young and elderly too
may know of my love and sing my praises."
He provided the people who had the skill and the vision
and guided them through the planning permission.
To his peoples great joy, in the year seventy two
God breathed life into the bricks and the mortar.
And fifty years on it still houses his people
Who pray for his mercy, and sing of his glory,
know His compassion and learn of His word,
Whilst aiming to be like Jesus our Lord.

Testimonies

The Horton Story
Ken's Story.

My first contact with Meadgate Church came by dropping off and collecting my children Paul and Carol when they attended Sunday School which was held in a local house.

I became more involved when my son Paul was a member of various youth groups and I helped with their activities by providing transport and supporting functions held at the Church and elsewhere.

About 30 years ago I decided to go to an evening Communion Service with my wife Wendy and soon afterwards made my commitment to serve Jesus. I became leader of the Men's group, did youth work, took part in services and generally supported the Church, all of which I greatly enjoyed.

To conclude, life is not all plain sailing but we have a Rock we can always rely on.

Wendy's story.

My first connections with Meadgate Church were being invited to a "Young Wives" group who held their meetings in the local school and hearing about Sunday School who met in a home locally to which I sent my children Paul and Carol.

When services began to be held in the school, we went along to those. It was a joy to move into the Church Building in 1972. It was not until 1973 that I committed my life to Jesus and have had the privilege of serving Him through Young Peoples work, Mums and Toddlers etc.

One of the special blessings has been the friendships formed over the years with many lovely people for which I thank God.

Recollections of a borrowed member of St. Mary's Church
A brief account from Louise Wright

When I first came to Great Baddow, I attended St. Mary's Church. I was wondering what I should do in the way of Christian work. I remember the Revd Michael Stedman asking me if I'd be interested in helping with a new project - a Sunday School on a housing estate where there was no church. It wasn't long before I was absorbed in the excitement of teaching in the primary school each Sunday morning.

Testimonies

I remember the preparations and planning for family services with Michael leading so skilfully that everyone got inspired.

I would like to say that throughout my years working in Africa, I have used Meadgate Church as an example. Children's work was not considered important, so I told them how teaching a few children in a home led to a new church. I hope they listened.

How I came to join Meadgate Church
God's plan for Melvyn Sach

My first recollection of the embryo Meadgate Church was in a field in between our row of houses and the Great Baddow bypass which was very new and not long opened (difficult to put a date to it but around 1966/7). There was a fete in that field which at that time belonged to our local farmer Mr Reg Spalding. My wife Jean and I wandered over and saw lots of stalls and people enjoying what we discovered was a fete run by the fledging Meadgate Church which at that time was held in the local school hall.

My clearest memory is a tall young man with a dog collar who I was told was the Revd David Evans. I later discovered he was the first Curate appointed at St. Mary's Church with special responsibilities for Meadgate. He was married to Rita and they were in the Parish from 1965-1968 living at 55 Longfield Road. We therefore had a sketchy idea of something going on in Meadgate in the way of church activities.

Jean and I moved to Meadgate on 1st August 1963 and were members of Springfield Baptist Church. In fact we were very involved in the church being among other things Sunday School Teachers. I was also a Lay preacher and a Deacon.

Our interest in Meadgate Sunday School was aroused one day by a visitor to our house. It was Mr Terry Gilder taking part in a house to house visitation campaign. He told us of the weekly children's meetings in the day school of which he was the Superintendent. In addition we were told of Family Services on the first Sunday of each month. When Terry heard we were teaching in a Sunday School in Springfield across the river, he said "You are needed here".

That was the first challenge we had that perhaps we should be serving God in our own district rather than walking or cycling one and a half miles into Springfield. However we carried on going to Springfield but the next big challenge that God may be calling us to a change in direction came on Good Friday 1969. On that day we felt we wanted to go to church but our own church didn't have a service on that day.

Testimonies

We therefore decided to go to the morning service at St. Mary's, Great Baddow. Little did we know that would trigger off an eventual change to our service to the Lord.

After that Good Friday service, we filed out behind others all shaking hands with the clergyman. When it came to our turn we were warmly greeted by the the Revd Michael Stedman although we didn't know who he was until then. After initial introductions, we told him a bit about ourselves and why we had come. On hearing of our experience as Sunday School teachers, he told us of the need for more helpers in the work at Meadgate. We went home that Good Friday somewhat challenged.

Not long after that first meeting, Michael Stedman appeared on our front doorstep. He was determined to quicken our initial interest in what was going on at Meadgate. To use footballing parlance, he was speculating in the transfer market. Not long after that we were invited round to 55 Longfield Road to meet Mike and Gill for a chat. We were intrigued by his office at the bottom of the garden which was a converted garden shed. I think from then on we felt the call. It would be difficult to leave our church at Springfield Park, but the call proved irresistible. At that time there was a monthly family service in the local school hall. We went along to some and were greatly impressed. The intervening weeks of each month, the Sunday School would meet in the school and we were impressed by the large number of children who attended. We were excited by the prospect of working in our own area and felt a realisation of why the Lord had moved us to Meadgate six years earlier.

Jean and I talked to our Pastor at Springfield Park and he said he felt God might be calling us and would give his and the church's blessing for a transfer. From then on we tendered notice that we would throw in our lot with Meadgate at the beginning of January 1970. We began to lay down the work we were doing at Springfield in preparation for this new sphere of service at Meadgate Church which was, we believe, God's will and it's a move we have never regretted.

How we left Springfield Baptist Church to join Meadgate
Account of Jean Sach's journey led by God's hand.

It was Good Friday morning 1969. There was no service at the church where Melvyn and I were members so we decided to go to St. Mary's Church in the village of Great Baddow. It was there that we first met Michael Stedman. He seemed very interested when we told him we were members of a local Baptist Church and we lived on the Meadgate estate.

Immediately after Easter, we went away for a few days holiday and shortly after our return home, there was a knock on the door. It was Michael.

Testimonies

We invited him in and he promptly told us about the Sunday School and Family Services, also the Wives Group, all held at this time in the Meadgate Junior School. He told us of the large number of children and the desperate need for more teachers in the Sunday School and asked us if we would consider helping.

At this time we were committed members of our own church. Melvyn was a Deacon and very involved and I was a Sunday School teacher and our own children Christine and Carol both attended the Sunday School. It would be very hard for us to leave such a thriving fellowship. Everything was there to help our children grow in Jesus. Besides all our friends were there, but it was a challenge and we could see that Meadgate needed our help more.

We thought and prayed a lot about it and gradually we were led to believe firmly that God had provided us with a house on Meadgate for a purpose and that was to serve Him in the Church where we lived. So in January 1970 we both started teaching in the Sunday School at Meadgate and soon after that resigned our membership at the Baptist Church, committing our lives to the Lord's service here on Meadgate.

It has been a privilege and joy to be part of the work on Meadgate for the past 40 years. We have seen many changes, experienced times of excitement, encouragements and joy and there have been times of disappointment and sadness. The Lord has given us so many lovely friends who have been such a help to us both in the church and in our own personal family life.

We thank God for the way he has blessed us all and trust Him for the future to do so much more, praying we will all be channels of His love drawing people to Him on the Meadgate estate.

To Him who by means of His power working in us, is able to do so much more than we can ever ask for or even think.
To God be the glory in the church and in Christ Jesus for all time.

The Beginnings of Meadgate Play Group
Betty Mead recalls.

My husband Tony and I moved to Meadgate with our one year old son Darron in September 1961. Houses were still being built around us, the shops and school yet to be completed. Our nearest church was St. Pauls in Beehive Lane. Four years later the school finally opened in time for Darron to attend. He also joined the Sunday School which was held in the school hall. Subsequently the Family Service was introduced. I was able to attend this along with Darron's three year old sister Cheryl.

Testimonies

I also joined the "Young Wives" Group (now named Cameo) which was held fortnightly in the school where I met other Christian ladies. As my daughter approached school age, I began to consider how I could fill the void left when both children were away at school. I looked at the possibility of retraining to work with children which had always been my ambition. My earlier occupation had been in Accounts (Book keeping).

It was pure chance that I spotted a small advertisement in the local paper regarding a Pre-School Playgroups Course which excited me, yet I was very apprehensive. Amazingly a few days later I received a phone call from a friend who urged me into applying. All my excuses for not doing so were overcome. In 1968 we both completed the course: so what next?

Around this time plans were being made to build the church on Meadgate with the hopes for a Playgroup. A member of the committee having heard of my training, mentioned my name. Thus I was invited to meet the Revd Jack Kingham. Resulting from this interview it was arranged for me to gain practical experience with St. Mary's Playgroup with a view to starting up our own group at Meadgate. However, another four years elapsed before the building was finally completed during which time our third child Anton was born.

At last our church was built and it was all systems go to get the playgroup set up to open in September 1972. I gathered an amazing team of trained helpers and we had tremendous support from the Church family and friends.

The group went from strength to strength with 25 under-fives on the register. The highlight of our year was always the Nativity performances, open evenings, outings, and fund raising events involving the parents whenever possible

It was a very fulfilling time for me and I believe it was the Lord who prepared and led me to this work. Sadly the playgroup closed in 1999 having served the purpose the Lord had for it.

Remember how the Lord led you all the way
Deuteronomy Chapter 8:2
Marion Bishop. Her recognition of God's guidance.

John my Husband had been accepted to work at Writtle Agricultural college as it was known in days gone by- one condition being that we re-located to Chelmsford. I remember John coming back to Colchester and saying "I think I have found a house for us". And so it was part of God's plan for us that we purchased 25 Spalding Way from Richard and Adrian Wilson, Christians whose home was used to house the ever growing Sunday School on Meadgate estate.

Testimonies

I recall a visit from Terry Gilder; Sunday school leader, and subsequently joined the Sunday School which was by now meeting in the Day School. Canon Kingham, the vicar, set the scene for the Wives Group. I recall the meeting of ladies who had come together for this purpose. I remember the Vicar saying that no-where else would this diverse group be found other than in the church. Rita Evans, wife of David, curate of St. Mary's was there and through Rita's suggestion that the natural way to conclude a Christian meeting the practice of closing our time with a Christian message was born. This has long since stayed with me. Rita our first leader was soon followed by Gill Stedman and then myself. All praise to Jill Smith-Hughes who continues to lead Cameo today. Tear Fund lunches became part of Church life. We served soup, bread and grated cheese, it went further this way. Twice a month enjoying great support from the Play Group staff, bread for Tear Fund was also available delivered by "the Church lady on her bike".

Alongside Wives Group, Senior citizens flourished and it was the Revd Peter Nicholson who suggested that monthly Bible study for senior citizens be brought into the main meeting and the first Thursday of the month was a devotional meeting. According to my husband I was the only apprentice senior citizen he had ever known. I'm learning the hard way. Then there was Bible study for us led by Diane Nicholson -they were happy helpful times -I still hold dear the verse Pat Davies gave me when we moved away. "I will lead the blind by ways they have not known, along unfamiliar paths I will guide them" (Isaiah 42:v16). This continues to be true, God is just the same today! "I will never leave you or forsake you" (Joshua 1:v5) and the people said "We too will serve the Lord because He is our God" (Joshua 24:v18).

The call of John Adams to Meadgate
Anna Adams relates it to us:-

In the autumn of 1976 we had returned from quite a difficult time of ministry where John had been a chaplain in Dusseldorf in Germany. The friends we were staying with suggested we visit Jack Kingham and we came to Great Baddow to speak to him and were excited by the opportunity to minister at Meadgate. Shared ministry and particularly shared church leadership was very important to John and one of his great joys was to work with Bill and Melvyn as church elders and seeking together God's direction for the way forward for the church.

As we look back we are thankful for the rebuilding God was able to do in our lives and the reaffirmation of God's calling to Ministry. As we moved on to join the European Christian Mission in 1980 to minister in Austria, it was with Meadgate Church totally behind. Their support and prayer and encouragement at that time meant that our friends at Meadgate have always held a very special place in our hearts.

Testimonies

My earliest recollections of Meadgate Sunday School
(the forerunner of Meadgate Church.)
Peter Hill

I remember my parents, Doris and Bill Hill, discussing the prospect of holding the Sunday School at our house; 12 Marney Close, Great Baddow. I would have been 10 years of age. We had moved there from Wickford at Easter time 1962. My 11th birthday was in March 1963. (I started at Rothmans Junior School for the final term of that school year.) The process of starting a Meadgate Sunday School, from the initial idea to its fruition must therefore have happened between Easter 1962 and the summer of 1963.

Apart from Chelmsford itself, there were only two churches in the area:
*St. Mary's, Great Baddow on the edge of the village towards the Hanningfields, and
*St Paul's in Beehive Lane, on another edge of Great Baddow, towards Galleywood.

My Mother must have felt, and the view must have been shared by others, that the nearest alternative Sunday School was too prohibitive a distance from Meadgate for most people with young children. Many young families had moved into the new Meadgate estate, but not so many people had cars in those days, and bus services were not as numerous as they have since become.

The Meadgate and Longmead estates were in their infancy. In fact building was still going on. I remember writing in a school essay later on at Grammar School, that I had spent part of my school holidays helping (or perhaps hindering) the builders.

I do not remember the lead up to the decision to start a Sunday School on Meadgate, or how it was approved by the Church. I remember Reverend John (Jack) Kingham, a tall kindly man who was Vicar at St. Mary's Church at that time. My recollection is that he was very supportive of what my Mother felt she was being called to do, and believe he must have been instrumental in the final decision.

As far as I remember, my Mother had not had any experience of any form of teaching, apart from as a parent to her then two children, myself and my sister Jenny. For this reason, I imagine the Reverend Kingham would have asked Terry and Beryl Gilder, to be a part of the project. Terry and Beryl, a husband and wife team who lived in Great Baddow, were both school teachers by profession and were active Christians. Terry, Beryl and my Mother are the original three Sunday School teachers in what is now Meadgate Church.

Testimonies

I am told, (though I did not remember) that for the first three months or so, Meadgate Sunday School was held in the house of close neighbours Frank and Norma Monk, whose house backed on to the side of ours. They lived at No. 250 Meadgate Avenue. Frank and Norma had made their gracious offer because in the summer of 1963, two events occurred to affect the planning for the launch of Meadgate Sunday School. One was the happy occasion of the birth of my brother Jeff in July. The other was the illness of my Grandfather, (my Mother's Father). He had moved in with us at about that time when his illness became terminal, and sadly he died on the 3rd November 1963.

Note: I always felt that my maternal Grandfather must have been a key element in my Mother's journey to becoming a committed Christian. My earliest recollection was that he scoffed at the prospect, but I clearly remember his face when he escorted her to the Bishop of Bradwell on the occasion of her Confirmation. It was the face of pride that a Father has when he escorts his daughter down the aisle on her wedding day. My Mother , being the first Christian in our family, initially had to endure the scepticism and only begrudging support of her closest family members in those early days. My Grandfather's face that day made me aware of God's grace and the significance of the Christian ministry, one that despite my rock solid faith, I have never felt worthy enough to follow.

When eventually, Sunday School started at 12 Marney Close, I remember having to be up early each Sunday, when I would much rather have stayed in bed a while longer. I had to take our dog "Skipper" for his morning walk and be back in time for breakfast. My Father was instrumental in the Sunday School preparation process and his support for my Mother was unfailing, as it has always been.

At that time he was not a committed Christian - that came later, so it would definitely have been a major inconvenience to him too, (like it felt for me). Everything was timed to the minute as I recall, and breakfast was speedily followed by the washing up, then the clearing up and hoovering of the house ready for the arrival of parents bringing their children for Sunday School. This would have been around 10.15 to 10.20am for a prompt 10.30am start. In the early days I was apprehensive when I saw parents turn up who I had seen while out playing on the estate up to that point. I hoped I had never misbehaved in their vision such that now they would be able to report me. Thankfully I was never embarrassed in that way, so either I was never that bad or they were too kind.

Testimonies

The hoovering was an important part of the process because the children's pews were the stairs. The early part of the service would have Terry leading from just inside the front door, with his congregation (including me) along the ground floor hall and up the stairs. Later in the hour, the group would be split into three according to age, with Terry taking the older children, Beryl the middle group and my Mother the younger ones. They used the kitchen, lounge and one of the bedrooms. I do not remember where I went at this point because even at 11 years of age, I was older than the rest of the children and did not take part in the second period of the service.

This continued for what seemed like a long period of time, until with many new members joining, the house was no longer big enough. Meadgate had generated so many new children that a new school was built in Mascall Way. Arrangements were made to transfer the Sunday School to the school premises and as far as I remember, this continued until Meadgate Church was built.

The new Church had been a long time in the making with many obstacles to overcome. When building commenced, it meant that one of my well-used bad weather routes for walking the dog was no longer going to be available to me. Before then, there was a hallway that ran between the shops and the rear of the building at the corner where the Church entrance now sits. In this hallway, were several cycle sheds on either side built into the structure, for the use of the people living in the flats above. I remember using that hallway many times as a way to get some respite, just for a minute, from the rain, and in the winter, the bitter cold.

And so from 1963 to 2013, Meadgate Church (which began with three Sunday School teachers and I believe 3 children on that first day, has grown to be a major influence on so many lives. It has its rightful place in Great Baddow. Those people who have helped it begin, nurtured its growth and helped it become the crucial focal point for the Christian and the wider community will surely be blessed. Not least of these is my Mother, with my Father's loving support, the wisdom of her wider Christian family and of course, God's calling.

My Meadgate Church
Jenny Burlington

These days it is very fashionable to "plant churches". Back in 1963 there was no such thing. Nevertheless, this is exactly what my Mum did. She planted the "mustard seed" that has become Meadgate Church. I feel that I could write a book myself about my life at Meadgate but I will leave that to her and try and condense my story into as few words as possible.

Testimonies

I was 6 years old when my Mum started the Sunday School in our house in Marney Close. The earliest memory I have is of sitting on the stairs whilst Terry Gilder counted the number of children present, to see if there were more than last week. If there were, then he would literally "break a record" it was such fun. We all loved that bit.

It was not long before we grew too big for our house and started meeting at Meadgate School. There was such a lovely atmosphere there, especially when we had the monthly family service. Parents, mostly non-Christians, would come regularly and the school hall soon became full. Tea and coffee was served in the kitchen area after the service and relationships were soon forged.

Everybody involved was so committed to the work and served so sacrificially. When I think about commitment, I think about people like Terry and Beryl Gilder, Melvyn and Jean Sach and my Mum and Dad (who wasn't even a Christian to start with) and eventually Michael and Gill Stedman who gave themselves so completely to this work over so many years. Every event was made all the more difficult because we didn't have our own building. Yet despite this, we had Sunday School outings, Christmas parties, summer fetes, rummage sales and more besides. I don't think that there was ever so much accomplished by so few.

I loved every part of it. I don't ever remember thinking that I wish I didn't have to go to church. Everything was such fun. The Sunday school outings to Walton-on-the-Naze, the Christmas parties, even the rummage sales were fun!. I think every event was fun because there was such a feeling of working together. Meadgate was and is such a special place. It was a very secure environment to grow up in and discover your faith. There were such good role models and above all such love. It really felt like family.

I think these early years really created a firm foundation for me to build my faith on. Later, as a teenager, I suddenly found that I was alone as far as other teenagers were concerned. There was no youth group for me. I went from Sunday School, to Sunday School teacher at the age of 15. I was desperate to be confirmed so that I could do this. Michael Stedman, who would have preferred me to be 16, got so worn down by my constant pleas that he relented and I joined the young people at St. Mary's to do the confirmation course. I think that this jump into adult Christian service really helped me to grow and mature as a Christian and it was easy to follow the great example set by those who had guided me so well during my childhood years. Surrounded by people who loved and prayed for me, I developed a faith that has been very deep in me all of my life.

Testimonies

Even my wedding was a huge church affair. I would really have loved to be married at Meadgate, but there was no license for weddings and as it turned out it would not have been big enough anyway. The service at St. Mary's was packed with our fellowship and friends. The singing was amazing and the support of all the church really overwhelmed me. The reception was at Meadgate and everybody pulled out all the stops to create a wonderful wedding breakfast at extremely short notice. I remember the day as a fantastic occasion, made really special by the love and support of my church family.

As an adult, I left Meadgate for a period of time and returned some years later. Once back in the fellowship, I had the opportunity to serve for a time running the Junior Church and toddler group as well as helping at Playgroup. Running the Junior Church was a time of great spiritual growth and maturity for me. It was during this time that I discovered my love of studying the Word and desire to share it with others. I hope and pray that God will develop this further, but I am so grateful that I had the time at Meadgate to undergo what I see as my training.

Meadgate Church is a very different church today, but I believe it is still as special. There is still such love and commitment and a safe environment for people to discover their faith and gifts and grow in them. During my time there, I have laughed and cried and others have laughed and cried with me. I have made lifelong friends who have supported me through all my ups and downs and I consider myself so fortunate to have been part of this wonderful work of God.

The influence of Meadgate Church.
Jeff Hill
Learning, growing and ministering as a Christian.

I have been a part of the Christian community of Meadgate Church since its foundation as an expression of the Sunday School movement in the 1960's.

As a child, the growing community gave me a sense of belonging. According to one faith development specialist this is the most important experience a child can have of Christian Community. The leaders achieved this through a vibrant Sunday School programme with the later addition of the popular family service. Bible stories were taught using visual aids and drama. I can remember waving furiously at the congregation when cast as the evil King Nebuchadnezzar.

The Sunday School gave me over a number of years, a thorough Biblical knowledge of the stories contained within scripture. The sense of community was widened to include outings, often on a coach to places like Walton-on-the-Naze, Greenwoods House (Stock) and Hylands Park. Here the Christian community played together and these experiences created bonds of love and peace.

Testimonies

What the community did well was to cater for young people at every stage of their development. There was the Pathfinder group providing a mix of games and teaching. By the time confirmation classes were held in the parish I had a clear understanding of what evangelical Christian faith was about and the need for a personal commitment to Christ, which I made during the mission visit of the "In the Name of Jesus" team. The ministry of Russ and Chris Cooper, who built a work with young adults, was highly influential from about the age of 17-22. The Sunday night meetings were the bread and butter ministry to our group of "Wayfinders" but their vision to inspire us was aided by many important national initiatives such as Green Belt festival, Spring Harvest, Earth Invaders and the Billy Graham Mission England project of 1984. I was beginning to discover great purpose in the Christian life, a call to spreading the good news was emerging through these experiences.

From 1985 onward, the relationship I enjoyed with Meadgate Church as a community changed from being a place where I learnt and was given space and freedom to grow as a Christian to one where I was given freedom and space to minister. They say a prophet is without honour in his home town, but after a year out experience of evangelism, I was reintegrated into the fellowship then commissioned as an evangelist.

Quite why this Church was able to allow a young person to mature and develop from within its ranks is an unusual story in itself, but they were able to do it. The Church committed sacrificial funds, time and energy to helping me set up a ministry which was, at times, frustrating but also fruitful.

The church and its leaders remained supportive of my ministry through difficult times as well as positive times. We travelled on many evangelistic adventures together over a nine year period including outreach through the youth club, Christmas drama in the streets, the Great Baddow Festival of Faith programme and the 2290 series of evangelism training weeks which Meadgate hosted. *(This was an evangelism programme for trainee street workers using sketch boards. It was devised by Hugo Anson. It was called 2290).*

Eventually God was to lead me away from my home church to study, recharge batteries, and develop a new vision for my life. But still this community of Christians have remained dear friends and partners in the Gospel and whenever I return with my family, we sense a warm welcome and unbreakable affinity.

Testimonies

Memories
Denise Hom

My first memories of Meadgate Church are not actually of Meadgate Church. When I was very young, I remember attending family services at Meadgate Primary School. This was where the meetings were held when they outgrew the family home it originally started in as a Sunday School. I can vaguely remember a brave man standing at the front with his guitar to lead the singing and then trooping out of the hall to the kitchen area where us children would have our lessons.

When the current building had opened I joined the youth group at about the age of 13 or 14 and there I made many friends I still have today. The youth group, led by Chris and Russ Cooper, was instrumental in my coming to faith and gave me wonderful times of fun and fellowship. The energy and enthusiasm Chris and Russ put into everything they did and some of the crazy things they came up with gave us all experiences we will never forget. I later became a Sunday School teacher myself and joined the music group, and it was through the friendships made at Meadgate and God's loving hand that I eventually met my husband to be and we are this year celebrating 25 years of marriage.

Meadgate Church has been part of my life for such a long time; through all the major events of my life; childhood, marriage, parenthood, and it has always been there with its friendship and love to support me when needed. The love and support it offers the local community has been appreciated by many over the years and hopefully with God's Grace it will go on for many years to come.

John Hom

I first heard about Meadgate Church after meeting Jeff Hill (Doris' son) at a Christian Conference in Derbyshire back in 1983. The year after I coincidentally got a job in Chelmsford, looked Jeff up, and started coming to Meadgate Church. I made some good friends whilst there, the best one being Denise whom I married a few years later. I sometimes think if that chance meeting in Derbyshire was coincidence, or was it God leading the way? Either way, it led me to my wife and many years of a happy marriage. Over the years, the church has seen many changes, and many ups and downs. Nonetheless, I have always felt that the Lord wants a church there, and He wants us there in amongst the community. Meadgate Church itself has become a significant part of my life and been a major contributor to my faith and life as a Christian.

Testimonies

Walking down the road
Allan Bell

One Sunday many years ago I was walking down the road, Meadgate Avenue, on the way to church with my daughter Natalie, then about fourteen. As we passed by a man digging at the front of his garden he stopped and said, 'Good morning. I hope you don't mind me saying something. I know you've had a hard time getting divorced and that; these things get about. But I'd really like to say how much I admire you and your daughter walking down to church every Sunday. I really wish you well.'

The mission statement of Meadgate Church is 'Aiming to be like Jesus'. When the Samaritan woman he met at the well (John 4.7), who had been divorced five times met him, she became his evangelist to the local city and crowds came out to see him. She was the only person he told directly who he was, and he even offered her baptism with the Holy Spirit ('living water'). 'Aiming to be like him' isn't a bad objective for any church, acting as a well in the local neighbourhood, where people can come to meet Jesus and his followers and be offered the gift of the Holy Spirit, whatever their history or background. As far as Meadgate Church is setting an example of how to do that then it could end up offering a worthy model to many others, to the greater glory of God.

I found the Lord at Meadgate Church
Joan Hammond's testimony.

My daughter Sue came home from school one day and asked if she could go to Sunday School with her friends. It was to be held in the local school which she attended. They had apparently been told that there was to be a Sunday School and along with others she was invited to attend.

After a few Sundays went by, Sue told us that my husband and I were to come with her the following Sunday as there was to be a Family service which meant that parents were invited. For a time my husband and I continued to attend the Family Services until the time came when the new church was built. My husband decided that church would be a bit heavy for him and sadly he didn't continue. Sue stayed at Sunday School and I began attending regularly and still do all these years later.

Now more than 40 years later, my husband was on the 24/7 prayer chain, due to stay in hospital with severe back pain. As he lay waiting for the ambulance, he said "Yes" to Jesus as we both agreed that we can be together in heaven as well as here on earth. "Praise the Lord". Now after prayers and treatment, his back pain has gone. The Lord has blessed him with a second chance. "Hallelujah".

Testimonies

The Lord's plan for my family
Doreen Thompson shares her experience.

Although my parents were not church going people, I was always sent to Sunday School as a child and later, as I grew up, I attended church as regularly as wartime conditions would allow. Once married I became a quite active member of our local church.

In 1970, with a toddler and two older children, we moved to Great Baddow and I attended St. Mary's church for a while, but although Jack and Nancy Kingham were lovely, I never really settled here. Whilst looking for something I could usefully do with a toddler, Mrs Kingham suggested I contact Betty Mead with a view to helping with the Playgroup that would be established when the new Meadgate Church Centre was opened.

Eventually when Alison was about four years old, the new church and playgroup opened and I joined Betty, Jean, Janet and Janice in helping the children learn and have fun. Soon after this we moved from the other side of Baddow to Longmead Avenue, by which time I had ceased to attend church at all.

One day during our coffee break, Jean Sach asked me about this and suggested I give Meadgate a try. This I did taking my two daughters with me, my 18 year old son not being interested in church going. The girls joined Sunday School which seemed to have a vast number of children lead by Melvyn Sach (Superintendent) with Doris Hill leading the younger ones. The church itself had a fairly small congregation, but everyone was very friendly, and soon we felt at home. I also joined the Wives Group (now CAMEO) and thoroughly enjoyed all the activities. I became a regular worshipper at Meadgate and still am. Derek, my husband, seeing how much I loved it, decided to come along and see what he was missing. He came to love it as much as I did and we both felt that we were Christians.

As the years passed and our Curates and Vicars changed, we attended various meetings, courses and House Groups, learning more and more all the time. During Morning Service one Sunday, Peter Nicholson challenged us to stand and make a real commitment to the Lord. This we did and realised that, at last we had actually given our lives to Jesus. We had never experienced a "blinding revelation", it had just grown on us over the years and it had taken a direct challenge to make us realise what our lives were all about.

I am glad to say that both our girls Mandy and Alison are committed to Christ and it is a great joy that Alison and her husband Darron, (Betty Mead's son) are also members of Meadgate Church. I have a great deal to thank Jean Sach for.

Testimonies

What Meadgate Church means to me
Jill Smith Hughes

Meadgate Church has been very dear and precious to me and my family for not far off 40 years.

My husband and I moved from Manchester in 1974 when Tom was promoted to a post at Nat West in the City. We started to look for a church similar to the lively student-type church we had attended in Manchester, Holy Trinity, Platt.

After a little 'church shopping' we settled at St. Mary's in Great Baddow, but after a year, when Tom found he knew the then Curate of Meadgate Church, Tony Bishop, from student days helping on beach missions, we gradually transferred to Meadgate where they needed youth workers.

Our first daughter Angela, had been born in 1975, and she used to sleep very contentedly through after-church-Sunday evening meetings in our home. We were delighted to host these gatherings and were privileged to have Christine and Carol Sach and Jenny and Jeff Hill in that group, among other lovely young people.

In 1977, I found I was expecting our second child and in due course, attended anti-natal classes at St. John's hospital. It was here that I came across a delightful mum-to-be, Angela Knights, now Angela Buetow. We were familiar to each other, but puzzled as to where we had met before. After our daughters, Hannah for me and Carolyn for Angela, were born, we met up again at the church, at what was known then, as Meadgate Wives Group and realised that it was there and also at the Meadgate Toddlers group that we had already met. We have been dear, close, valued friends ever since and have shared the ups and downs, the joys and sadness's of life, prayerfully together.

Tom and I found that the style of worship, along with the strength of the incredibly supportive Church Family, really suited us and we put our roots down firmly. Tom was soon involved as an Elder and over the years, he enjoyed roles on the PCC, the DCC and the Deanery Synod. While the girls were young, I let Tom get involved mainly, but I gradually found that I could support the children's work in the 45 Club and I enjoyed helping with food preparation at church events and was guilty of quite a few examples of silliness, when entertainment was put on. Bit by bit, God led me to serve Him for several terms of office, on the DCC and that, along with the MLT, has been such rewarding work, to see His guidance, provision and answer to prayer over the years.

Testimonies

I was surprised, one day in the late 70s, to be approached by Marion Bishop, the Leader of the Meadgate Wives Group, who felt very strongly that God was telling her to give up that role and that I should take over. This amazed me, as I was a fairly new member and, until then, I had found a ladies only gathering rather strange. I was to change my mind about that very quickly and realised just how much ladies benefit from each other's company, gathering together regularly and supporting each other in friendship and fellowship. That was amazingly the best part of 35 years ago and CAMEO ('Come and Meet Each Other'), as the group is now called, has played a huge part in my life and is a joy, privilege and a priority for me. Angela and I have worked together in this calling, with a brilliant team of dedicated ladies, throughout that time and we thank God for all our members and ask Him to guide us in our communication of His love in this setting.

We have been greatly blessed at Meadgate throughout the years, by our Clergy and, as Tom always used to say, "We've had the right man, at the right time in the church's life", and we have always thanked God for the brilliant leadership, wisdom, teaching, caring and pastoring we have enjoyed at Meadgate.

Meadgate Church has been so central to the life of my family and I thank God for every aspect of it. We move from one exciting period to another and yet the stability underpinning everything is the love, help, support, concern, kindness and prayer-backing shown by our dear Brothers and Sisters in Christ! I can testify to this, having lost my dear Tom just a year ago, and I can't imagine life without the love of our wonderful church family- thank you everyone! I am so delighted and thankful that God guided us to Meadgate all that time ago!

Testimonies

My History of Meadgate Church
As told by Angela Buetow.

My late husband and I moved from West Midlands in the 1976 summer heat wave. I had a 2 year old boy and desired to find a mother and toddler club and make friends as I knew no-one here. I heard there was such a club in a local church somewhere nearby so I went into the Mormon church near to me on Baddow Road to enquire, but it was not there. However, a lady said perhaps it was the church in the Meadgate estate and kindly walked me there!

I found out when the club met at Meadgate Church and went along, arriving early. As I walked into a big empty room, I stood and looked around and heard in my mind the words "This is going to be your home". This was a strange phenomenon to "hear words" and it made an impact on me, although I did not understand why I heard it, yet I have always remembered.

I began attending Toddlers' club weekly with my little boy and made a few friends amongst the mums. The leaders were very kind and each week one would speak a few words in the tea break about God loving us and that His Son Jesus died for us and explained what the Bible said about things to which we mums could relate. I found this interested me.

I became pregnant and attended childbirth classes at the hospital and found a pleasant lady call Jill who seemed somehow a little familiar but we could not tie down where we might have come across one another. We had both lived in other parts of the country.

Nearing the end of the pregnancy in December 1977, I was invited by a neighbour to again attend an evening social group for ladies held at Meadgate Church, where we enjoyed listening to an interesting topic from a visiting speaker. It was a couple of weeks before Christmas and the speaker was Canon Kingham from St. Mary's, Great Baddow. His talk really spoke to me as it was all about "Mary being heavy with child" and that was exactly my physical state at that moment! He spoke about her baby being born in the stable and that it was part of God's plan for the world and for individuals too. A week later I was giving birth in St. John's Hospital, Chelmsford and was blessed with a beautiful little girl.

What joy! I had a lovely boy and now a girl! I felt so thankful to God as I lay there in the delivery room and could hear my new baby's voice. I was left on my own for a while and I felt an awareness of my sinfulness and God's wonderful goodness to me, which I felt I didn't deserve, and yet He had still blessed us with this lovely "pigeon-pair" (as my aunty said of the children).

Testimonies

I welled up with thanks and made a promise in my heart that from now on I would do all I could to please God and follow His ways.

The ladies' group heard of the birth and someone came with flowers. It touched my heart deeply that they barely knew me yet had shown me such kindness. As soon as I could I went back to the ladies' group (Meadgate Wives) and as I walked in I recognised Jill, the lovely lady who had shown me friendship at the childbirth classes. Amazing - it turned out that she was a member of this ladies' group and her baby girl had been born 3 weeks before mine. So that was where we had seen each other before! We wanted our new baby christened and I queried with the curate's wife at the ladies' club if they would do this in Meadgate Church (as it didn't look like a traditional church building). When she said "yes" I asked where the font was. "Oh we use a bowl" was her reply! Her husband, the curate John Adams had to visit us to arrange the christening service and it was then I said to my husband "I really want to start going to church every Sunday." I gave my life to Jesus about 32 years ago and the church has become my spiritual home.

Jill and I became good friends and our daughters used to play together. We have stayed committed to Meadgate Church and love God's family there. Our faith in Jesus has grown enormously and we have each been given more and varied responsibilities to serve God and help others come to know Jesus. God had His plan for us right from the time we both had baby bumps and met in the childbirth classes! For many years we have also enjoyed serving God in that same ladies' group who sent me flowers and which is now called CAMEO (e.g. Come and Meet Each Other). He started a process and I followed each time I heard his call.

Two years ago I had the sudden death of my husband; we were married 41 years. I found that through my deep faith and wonderful support and prayers of the church family I was really carried through that first year of bereavement. I was able to whole-heartedly praise and worship Jesus our Saviour because I knew my husband had opened himself to God the Holy Spirit on the last afternoon he was alive. He believed in Jesus but had never made a habit of church attendance. He was a great support to me so that I could spend time serving in the church, and when he was feeling unwell on that (unbeknown to me, last day), I asked him "God loves you, please will you let me pray and ask Him to bless you?" He had never agreed to be prayed over before but this time he allowed me to invite the Spirit of God upon him and thereby gave God permission to enter into his heart. That night the Lord decided to take him home to heaven. When I awoke in the morning I again "heard in my mind" words of the 23rd Psalm. The room was bright and I felt God's presence. I went downstairs and found him, looking very peaceful and I knew what had happened. I prayed and committed his spirit into the safekeeping of Jesus. My husband was safe in the care of the God in whom I trust. (Submitted by Angela Feb. 2010)

Testimonies

Our Move to Great Baddow 1977
June and Roy Davidson.

We spent our early years in South London, and moved to a historic village near Maidstone. We lived there for 13 years bringing up our children Mark and Kathryn. Suddenly we had to move to Essex due to Roy's change of employment.

What a difficult time a move is! There is a real sense of loss of friends, familiar surroundings and of course a Church we had known for those 13 years plus the tasks God had given us to do there. Once we had arrived and settled in our task was to find a Church. We went along to St. Mary's but it was different to our church in Aylesford, so we looked around and in the Parish Magazine we saw Meadgate Church Centre. We didn't know the area, and when we set out to find a steeple in Meadgate, we were confused as there wasn't a sign of a church. We phoned the then curate, the Revd Tony Bishop and said "where is your church?" When he explained that it was in the shopping car park we were a little surprised and curious.

When you move, what do you look for when trying to settle into a new church? We knew we wouldn't find a church quite like our old church, which was an ancient church built on the Pilgrim's Way, but we wanted an Anglican Church that was Bible based, friendly and where we could use the gifts we had used over so many years, and more besides if possible. We went along to a Service at Meadgate and found a very different style, but a place we felt comfortable in. We were made so welcome and during the days ahead we had at least six people from the Church come to visit us, and a very Christian lady who helped us in so many ways.

We hadn't been here very long before Jean Sach visited and had got to know we had helped in Sunday School and Bible class, and that was the start of a long journey into the continuing work of spreading the Good News of Jesus to children and young people. The voluntary youth team worked together and from 3 - 18 years and so many were involved from the beginning with Doris Hill to the older group led by Christine and Russell Cooper with too many helpers to name. Hopefully they will write their story.

What we also enjoyed about Meadgate was not only the sense of Worship and Glory to God but the fun we had. We enjoyed social evenings, barn dances (which helped us to get to know lots of people), New Year Get To-gethers enabling new folk to feel at home. This all gave a good sense of fellowship.

Testimonies

Of course the church which was quite small initially had worked so hard with the young people and a strong Sunday school, led by Melvyn Sach. The Sunday School had used the school, scout hut etc., and of course people's homes. As today the size of the building was and is a problem.

For me - June, the next step was Pathfinders which I co-led with Malcolm Cumming, and I get excited today when I see so many of those members still working for the Lord, some working in Ministry but also working in the Community. Many have moved away but have taken that love they have of the Lord with them.

We suddenly got to hear about Spring Harvest, and one year many of us went to a snow clad, wild weather Butlin's in Prestatyn. The weather was terrible, the Big Tent wouldn't stay up and had to be abandoned, but what fun we had, and the worship and teaching was so good it gave us all new insight. It also helped us because we met people from other parts of the country. The love of Spring Harvest went on for many years and so many people from Meadgate Church went, and it was a special time of fellowship and sharing.

One year they announced that Graham Kendrick who was very active at this time, writing beautiful hymns and being an excellent worship leader said that he wanted to organise a "March for Jesus" in the City of London. We hadn't a clue what this would be or who would be going, but we went to Chelmsford station and found a good contingent from Meadgate on the platform bound for London. There was only one problem, it was pouring with rain but we were not deterred - we had a wonderful day with thousands rather than hundreds attending - yes we did get soaked to the skin, but survived just the same. These marches went on for many years, in fact until the Millennium.

There were also local marches, and Meadgate Church marched round the parish to spread the love of the Lord to our local friends. Others in the church organised special events at the Annual May Fayre in Baddow, notably the "Glory Story" (written by Ishmael) and also a Victorian event! So much I could write about those days.

Meadgate Church has grown quite a lot since the early days, the style of worship has changed but the most important aspect is always that it is a Bible Based Ministry, teaching the love of the Lord and outreach. Since the days we were youth workers this is now different as a youth minister is employed to do the work, which is really helpful and a real asset to the youth work. We need to ensure that the next generation is well prepared to work hard for the Lord, making the church and family of God strong and secure by being made as welcome as we were when we first crossed the threshold. A smile, a welcome, showing someone new to a seat and linking them up with someone who is a member of the church is a wonderful way to achieve this.

Testimonies

Our Christian journey of service continued, Roy as treasurer for many years and June church warden. Our journey will continue, possibly in a very different way, but we will always remember the welcome we received when we first moved to Great Baddow, finding a church that gave Glory to God.

Meadgate Church
Helen Kiff

My introduction to Meadgate church began shortly after I moved to Chelmsford with my family when aged 9 years. I had no previous experience of church but a new friend asked me along to Sunday School and I decided to give it a try. It was the beginning of my walk with God, amongst people who have demonstrated the love of God to me and my family over a number of years.

I have great memories of my teenage years within the church, enjoying sponsored Bible readings and midnight walks in Danbury, courtesy of Chris and Russ Cooper. The fellowship experienced during those times has been hard to beat and I am sure helped develop me as a person through those formative years. My time away at college gave me a greater awareness of the special place Meadgate held in my heart as it proved hard to find a church where I felt as comfortable as at Meadgate.

Like the majority of people I have been aboard the roller-coaster of life and have consequently experienced a variety of life's blessings and challenges. God has always provided the support I needed through the body at Meadgate with many long established friendships. It's hard to imagine life without those people God has firmly planted in my life. I trust and pray that I continue to be part of the fellowship at Meadgate for many years to come…..

Meadgate Church
Sue Beaver

In 1996 I moved back to Chelmsford with 3 small children. I came from a church background, mainly URC and Methodist, but had also become a member of the Church of Scotland whilst we lived there. I wanted to find a church where I felt at home but it had to be somewhere the children enjoyed the Sunday school.

We tried many churches in Chelmsford. I hated my first visit to Meadgate - the loud modern music, lots of welcoming people (I prefer to hide in the shadows), a service that was not my traditional "hymn sandwich" and we sat with the Buddies which to my shame made me feel very uncomfortable. (*The Buddies are a small group of Downs Syndrome people living in a communal home in Beehive Lane. They were collected and returned on Sunday mornings by Ken Horton whilst he was still able to and subsequently by Melvyn Sach until they were no longer able to attend*).

Testimonies

But the children all liked the Sunday School, so we started coming regularly and I have continued to do so for 17 years. I now love the Worship each week and really miss the Buddies. I have enjoyed being part of the church and playing a small part in some of its many activities. The older children have all stopped coming, but I pray they will return someday having had such a good start.

For me, I believe God brought me to Meadgate. I have learned so much about our loving God and the close relationship we can have with him. I have made many wonderful friends, some sadly no longer here, that have provided prayer and support for me over the years through life's ups and downs.

I cannot thank God enough for bringing me to this place.

My account of my years at Meadgate
Peter Nicholson

By mid-1980 I had been a curate at Christ Church, West Croydon for four years when Clive Sperring, the curate of St. Paul's, Great Baddow, rang me and asked if I was thinking of making a move. Clive was a friend from college days whom my wife Diane and I had introduced to Linda, a onetime member of the group I ran whilst I was in the RAF. They hit it off straight away and got married. I told Clive that I wasn't thinking of moving but he said that he would tell me about Meadgate Church anyway. He explained that it was an ecumenical experiment. Christ Church was experiencing building problems at this time and we were beginning to consider the possibility of joining up with the Methodists and becoming a Local Ecumenical Project with a shared building. Diane and I were due to visit some friends north of Chelmsford for a few days so we decided to call in and find out a bit more as to what an ecumenical project involved. To our surprise, we were given appointments not only with the curate John Adams, but also with Canon Jack Kingham, the Vicar of St. Mary's, Great Baddow, and some members of Meadgate Committee.

Over a couple of days, Diane and I felt a strong call to serve at Meadgate Church but there was one big problem - the curate's house. It wasn't big enough for us and two growing daughters, Sarah and Tracy. We needed a third bedroom. The Meadgate Committee told us that they would make it a priority to extend the house should we decide that I should become the next curate of Meadgate Church, so we accepted.

The day we moved, the scaffolding went up and in a very short space of time we had our third bedroom. Now it was time to get to grips with this rather unique ecumenical experiment call Meadgate Church. The sponsoring body was St. Mary's PCC and Meadgate Church had no formal links with any other denomination.

Testimonies

The idea was that people from any denomination could become members of Meadgate Church without having to change their denomination. The liturgy of the church was very relaxed and informal and the people came from a range of free church and catholic backgrounds. It was quite daring for its time, Bishop Trillo having told Jack Kingham just to "get on with it".

One day whilst rummaging around the wooden chalet at the end of our garden, I found a piece of A4 paper entitled, "A Draft Constitution of Meadgate Church" I tweaked it slightly to reflect how the church was currently operating and presented it to the Church Committee. I got the impression that they thought this new upstart of a curate was trying to tell them how their church should be run. Once I had had the chance to explain the origin of the piece of paper, everyone calmed down and we eventually agreed the draft. Now people had a piece of paper to explain how we operated.

The church was fed up with clergy only staying for a few years and then moving on. They asked if we would be prepared to stay at least five years which we agreed to do. In the end we enjoyed our time so much that we stayed 15 years. During that time, Meadgate Church became part of Great Baddow Team Ministry and I became Team Vicar. Because of the freedom to operate given by Jack Kingham, as "curate in charge", the change to Vicar status brought little change to how Meadgate Church functioned. However, we got a bigger house and I got a title.

During our time at Meadgate Church, we managed to expand the premises by renting and re-ordering unused storage space below the adjacent block of flats, so we had rooms for the Sunday School. In the mid 90's a group of us went up to Holy Trinity, Brompton on an Alpha Course training day and Alpha courses became part of the regular outreach of the Church. I held my first baptism by total immersion in the local school swimming pool followed by an hour's swimming for anyone who wanted to indulge. Emily Burlington was the one who was baptised.

For a time, we experimented with having monthly family services at the school. In the early days of the church large numbers met in the school, we were unable to significantly make it worthwhile to continue with the experiment. Under God's guidance, we developed a healing and deliverance ministry. Members included Sandra Southee, Angela Knights, Diane Chasmer and Marian Luketa. We saw the Lord Jesus regularly heal and set people free from the oppression and affliction of the enemy. We were also asked to go into houses and places to cleanse them of occult or disturbing activity and we saw the Lord do amazing things.

Testimonies

I well remember one man, John, (not a church attendee although his wife sometimes came along to church) who I would sometimes see outside his house and we would talk together. One day I encountered John outside his house and it became clear all was not well. He had been laying carpet and had badly strained his back. He was in a lot of pain, so I told him that if he came along to church on Sunday, we would be happy to pray for him and ask the Lord to heal him and take away his pain. I thought no more of it until John arrived at church. He told me that he wouldn't have come if his back had improved. I sat him in a wooden chair at the back of the church, so he had to endure both the service and pain in his back. Afterwards we took him into the ministry room, laid hands on him and prayed for healing. Before I realised what was happening, he bent down and touched his toes, then walked up and down the room exclaiming "I don't believe this, I don't believe this." He went home pain free, but then decided to move some heavy furniture and did his back in again. I think he must have been too embarrassed to come back for more ministry.

Another memorable event was when I led a lady to the Lord Jesus Christ in her home. After praying the prayer of commitment she said, "Is that all there is?" I than told her about the Holy Spirit. She stood up against one of the walls in her room whilst I laid hands on her head and asked the Holy Spirit to come and fill her. She gently slid down the wall under the anointing of the Holy Spirit, just as her husband walked past the open doorway. I never did find out what he made of that.

Diane and I were privileged to work with a great team of people and I especially appreciated having Melvyn Sach as both a Baptist and excellent preacher. He kept me on my toes as we sometimes differed theologically and this made me think things through more carefully.

We made good friends at Meadgate Church and we always look forward to returning for the occasional visit…

Our coming to Meadgate
The Revd Mones Farah

We arrived at Meadgate on the 10th of February 1998. It was a move of 300+ miles. It was a step that we have enjoyed thoroughly and one which has blessed us immensely.

I was born in the north of Israel and grew up in the town of Nazareth. Yes, yes I can hear you say. Is there anything good that comes from Nazareth? My answer has always been the same. Yes, at least two: the Lord and I. At the age of 19 I moved to the UK with the desire to study veterinary science, and settled in a small village in West Wales.

Testimonies

Through the testimony of my Welsh adopted Mum and the witness of the local Christian Church, an ardent atheist was found and rescued by Jesus. I came to faith in one of the Brecon renewal days on the 3rd of November 1984, and very soon after I felt a call to the ministry. I tried to ignore that sense of call, but whatever I did just failed. The Bishop of St David's at the time agreed to take me on as an ordinand with the words: 'I'll take a risk on you.'

In my first year at Trinity College, Bristol, I met Sally, and just before ordination at St David's Cathedral we were married. After ordination we moved for our curacy at Aberystwyth, followed by seven years in charge of the chaplaincy at the University of Wales, Lampeter.

It was at Aberystwyth and Lampeter that we had our daughters Elizabeth, Eleanor, Mary-Anne and our foster daughter Sarah The first three moved with us to Meadgate, while Sarah followed nine years later. At the end of our time at Lampeter we sensed that God was calling us to Meadgate. Although our application arrived two days late, we were given the opportunity of an interview, and later on the position of Team Vicar of the church where we have been for the last 15 years.

From our earliest days here, we felt that we belonged. We were and continue to be supported by a wonderful faithful body of believers. Through us together God has done amazing things among us, from refurbishing and expanding the building, to the growth of strong children, youth and adult ministries. Evangelism and outreach have been at the heart of the ministry of the church, and it is a constant delight to see the hand and work of God upon the ministry here.

God has done and continues to do amazing things here. We have received a fantastic spiritual foundation and body, on which, in partnership with our congregation's members, by the grace of God, we added to.

All that I am able to say is: His plans are good to those who trust him, and they are definitely yes and amen!

Testimonies

God's plan bringing me back to Essex.
Sally Farah

Being Essex born and bred, it should not have been surprising to return to my roots and take up the post of Vicar's wife at Meadgate church, but in actual fact it was.

After ten years of working in Wales, God drew me back to my home turf to become "Mrs Vicarage"(an endearing term which seems to have stuck), to a wonderful group of people. For some being given a nickname which so closely aligned them with their husband's job, would feel like a loss of identity and not be welcomed. But to be honest, I have loved being Vicar's wife at Meadgate. Perhaps because the church has given me nothing but support and encouragement in finding out just what "Vicar's wife" looked like for me with my own particular gift set.

Fifteen years ago when we first arrived, I was a different person. I liked to hide quite a lot, sitting right at the back of the church and shooting away at the first opportunity, but God has taken me on a journey of growth in all sorts of areas. Moving me through children's work, a puppet ministry to heading up training and discipleship in the church. He has developed my leadership and preaching gifting. To be working alongside my husband hand in hand with God has been such a joy, and having the people of Meadgate graciously cheering me on from the side-lines, has been a privilege for which I shall be forever grateful.

The Dixon family
Sarah Dixon

Many memories come unbidden to my mind; the painful memory of having to leave a body of people that I had loved and served in order to find the new place that God wanted us is now submerged in the loving acceptance I found at Meadgate. I have to write in terms of my family when I think of how we came to be here. Alan and I and our two children, Emily and James, were looking for a new church in the autumn of 2002. We were not concerned for ourselves but we wanted to find a place where our children would grow up safely in a Godly atmosphere - a church which displayed the character of Jesus and the love of God. After a few months of looking around, it was the children who suggested trying Meadgate Church and once we came we knew we had found what we were looking for. God has been so good to us as a family here -not only has it been a safe place to bring up our children, but it has been a place of love and support for Alan and myself as well.

Testimonies

Our whole family has been blessed over the years that we have been here in so many ways and we are thankful for the children and young people's work, for house groups, for the care that was shown me in the years when I was unwell, for the love and kindness of the many friends we have made here. I give thanks for the goodness of God that I have found here.

My Meadgate Testimony
Nadia

I thank God for bringing me to Meadgate Church. Meadgate Church is a treasure hidden which is so easy to miss. I have been in the church fully since October 2012.

I first came in on a Wednesday afternoon to try the drop-in worship session and was so blessed with the worship. The last 45 minutes were for intercession which was so heart felt prayer, full of meaning and I felt so easy to join in without fear that I am not one of them. My next port of call was the Friday morning intercession meeting. Again I was so welcomed like one of them and did not feel like a stranger and just connected in a way I could not explain. It was in one of the Friday meetings that one of the Ladies had a word of knowledge for me to join the school of ministry. They explained how it runs. I later spoke to Mones and was surprised that the school of Ministry was starting the following week. Seeing the materials that I was learning and that it needed practice I then felt it could only make sense to join that church in order to be able to have a chance to practice what I was gaining from the school of ministry.

BENEFITS;

There is the reality of God in this place. Every aspect of it has and is still changing my life in a great way. I have been in many different places of worship but have never come across God as clearly as at Meadgate Church.

Tools for aids: (Soaking, worshipping session, Sozo, praying ministry) very powerful and Spirit filled. God knows all and knows what He needs to do in, with and through me and I know that is being achieved. I always feel that presence of God/ the anointing with me for days after prayers. It is like being given a dose of antibiotic.

Church services. I love to attend all three church services on a Sunday because they are different and bring our God in a different way.

Testimonies

First service: I get to meet a lot of people in all age groups. I am able to join in prayers and the soaking before the service starts. By the time the service starts, I will be all plugged in and the flow of the Holy Spirit continues in me. I have seen Father God ministering to me in different ways in this service and using different aspects of the service from worshipping to the fellowshipping after the services. I need to be sensitive to the Holy Spirit.

The second service: It feeds me, a Bible study service where the word of God is explored with a lot of cross referencing, also I learn a lot of different things about the generation before because the majority members are a generation before mine. In passing they drop a lot of good tips about life and some aspects we seem to be overlooking today. Again this service with its laid back style prepares me for the final service of the day.

Final service: I am blessed when I attend this service for the following reasons:
1. The generation involved are being used by God to do His work.
2. The worship in the service.
3. The Word which is personal experiences and testimonies.
4. The demonstration of the power of God through prayers after the word. The Spirit of God is not limited to time in this service, just to follow and transform lives. One can never predict what will happen in this service, that is why I find it hard to describe it.

I truly thank God for bringing me to Meadgate Church. I am beginning to find some answer to life which I have been looking for a long time. I pray LONG LIVE MEADGATE CHURCH.

Meadgate Church
Wendy Fagg

I was welcomed into Meadgate Church at the age of 18. I enjoyed the sermons of Peter Nicholson and then Mones, they were very thought provoking. Peter taught me how to pray for healing.

When I was ill and in hospital, Meadgate folk visited me and prayed, sent cards and presents for which I was very grateful. When I was well the church supported and encouraged me. Mones continued the prayer ministry and the Alpha Course was great.

Once a group from Meadgate went to see a well know speaker on the subject of healing and we witnessed miraculous healing. Norwich City football ground was the venue. God still heals today. On visiting the church on October 6th, I had healing of my emotions when Angela prayed for me. Meadgate Church was and still is a caring and sharing family. Happy 50th Anniversary.

Testimonies

MEADGATE JUNIOR CHURCH *(Emma Smith to Doris Hill)*

Our young people richly deserve a mention in this book and I decided that the best way to approach this would be to give them a questionnaire and sign it with their Christian names only for their protection:-

1. Q   What do you think of the club for your age group?
   A   "I like that you get to socialise with other people" - *Alham, age 10*
   A   "Six Pack is epic and awesome" - *Cameron, age 10*
   A   "The Church has everything we need" - *Emily Jane, age 6*
   A   "We play lots of games" - *Jessica, age 7*

2. Q   What do you think of the building and facilities at the church?
   A   "There is enough room for everyone" - *Ella-Mae, age 10*
   A   "I like that we can use the building for school services" - *Sophie , age 10*
   A   "The building is open for many things" - *Anja, age 11*
   A   "There are good games consoles" - *Lino, age 6*

3. Q   What do you think of the atmosphere in Junior Church?
   A   "We all get along; We are like one really big family and the times we spend together are inspiring" - *Seraphina, age 12*
   A   "It's really nice and relaxed" - *Allesandra, age 12*
   A   "It is quite welcoming" - *Peter, age 10*

4. Q   What do you think of the atmosphere in our Sunday Service?
   A   "It is calm and relaxing and everyone is nice to be around"; "No-one expects you to do anything you don't want to"- *Meg, age 13*
   A   "It is a place where you can have a new laugh, also where you learn new and interesting stuff" - *Shana, 14*

5. Q   What have you learnt about through the church and its teaching?
   A   "I have learnt a bit about everything" - *Elyse, age 7*
   A   " I learn about the Bible" - *Tiffany, age 9*
   A   "I have learnt about the love that our God has for us, and why we are here, I have also learnt lots about the bible that I never knew before"
   — *Izzy, age 14*

Testimonies

Conclusion (*Doris Hill*)

Meadgate church has been my spiritual home and our members my spiritual family. My husband and I feel mightily privileged to have worshipped and served here now for fifty years. This year 2013 is our jubilee and we find ourselves elderly members now. We see an army of younger people carrying on the business of the church as well as the spiritual side of it. Truly we are blessed and will never cease to remember that God has been with us every step of the way so far and I know he will continue to do so as long as we are obedient and faithful to Him. There are so many carrying on His work and assisting Mones as he has the task of leading us and helping us to grow. We are still learning.

My hope is that as the church continues that the coming events will be recorded by someone so that future generations will know the history as the church continues to move on.

Many of us have grown older now but somehow we still feel needed and have found that the Lord still has a purpose for us. There was a time when Bill and I felt that our service was coming to an end, but it has not been so, but as we thought about that possibility, Bill found a poem by Thomas Hardy that really helped us to let go and let the younger people have their time. I would like to finish with this poem that may be of help to the next generation of elderly people who feel they are no longer wanted.

By Thomas Hardy

As newer comers crowd the fore we drop behind,
We who have laboured long and sore time out of mind
And keen are yet must not regret to drop behind

Chapter 12
Time Line

Note: The following events and dates have been abstracted from many sources and there are various gaps, which may be filled in as various other items are discovered or brought to mind.

1961
Building of council properties on Meadgate Estate begins on land acquired by Chelmsford Borough Council from Spalding farm. At this point there were no shops, no school no church, no by-pass road..

1962
Easter. Bill and Doris Hill arrive and settle in Marney Close with son Peter and daughter Jenny.

1963
August. Newly-wed teachers Terry and Beryl Gilder move into 507 Meadgate Avenue and play key roles in the development of Meadgate Church.
Sunday School, led by Terry and Beryl Gilder, opened in the home of Norma Monk. First children to attend were Trevor and Karen Walden, later joined by Peter and Jenny Hill, who were ill at the time of the first session.

November. Sunday School moved to the Hill's house and quickly grew in numbers, until a group of older children were moved to the home of Richard and Adrienne Wilson.

1964
Sunday School continues to grow in the Hill's home.

19th December. First family service with twenty people attending.

1965
April/August. Church obtains two ninety-nine year leases from Mr R.L. Spalding for land on which to build a 'church and premises'.

Summer. Arrival of David Evans (Curate at St Mary's) and his wife Rita, moving into the curate's house at Longfield Road, where their daughters Sarah and Kate were later to be born. David had responsibility for the church's work on the new Meadgate Estate.

Testimonies

1966

13th May. First meeting of the Meadgate Committee, set up by the Revd Jack Kingham to consider the building of a church on the Meadgate Estate. First idea was for a prefabricated building to be erected on a site near the Spalding farmhouse, but planning permission was not granted because of access problems. The Revd Kingham's minuted view, which won unanimous acceptance, was 'that we should seek to use it as a centre to meet the needs of people on the Meadgate Estate, so that our image should be one of service.'

8th July. Having been refused planning permission for the first site, the committee met to consider a second possible site at the bottom of Mascall's Way.

14th October committee meeting was told that the second site would probably be refused planning permission. The Meadgate Fund now held £1400, but it was understood that more would be required.

1967

10th January. Meadgate Committee meeting was told that planning permission for the Mascall's Way site was refused.

7th February. Meadgate Committee decided to investigate other sites and to try to rent school premises for Sunday School use.

14th March. Meadgate Committee was told that possible sites on land allocated for allotments behind Meadgate shops and at Whitehouse farm were being considered. Meadgate School premises plus a piano for Sunday School use were on offer for 18 shillings a session in summer and £1-0-6d in winter.

23rd April. First Sunday School held in a hired hall at Meadgate Junior School with about 100 children and 15 teachers. Later a monthly family service was introduced with increasing numbers of parents attending.

September. A rummage sale and an open air fete were held to raise funds.

15th November. The Revd Kingham proposed to the Meadgate Committee that the church should become a 'daughter' church of St Mary's. It was felt that the church should have flexibility of use, also accommodating 'the Darby and Joan club, nursery schools, clinics, youth groups, etc.
19th November. Sunday School anniversary service at Meadgate School.

Time Line

1968

Young Wives and Darby and Joan groups started.

16th February. Meadgate committee discuss erecting a Marley type prefabricated building on a site next to the British Legion hall.

22nd June. Fund-raising jumble sale held.

23rd June. Open air service held.

20th July. Summer fete held on Meadgate School playing field.

24th September. Arrival of the Revd Michael Stedman, the first Meadgate curate, and his wife Jill.

1969

14th July. Summer fete on Meadgate School sports field, with music by Chelmsford Silver Band.

4th November. Application for outline planning permission came before the Chelmsford Rural District Council.

11th November. Outline planning application approved. Next step submission of a detailed planning application.

Final layout of Church Centre decided. Drawings prepared in preparation for bye-law permission

1970

January. Advice sought on lease of site from Borough of Chelmsford. Melvyn and Jean Sach transferred to Meadgate Church from Springfield Park Baptist (where they had been Sunday school teachers and Melvyn was a deacon).

Derek and Christine Jeffrey moved away. (Derek had been on the Committee. He organized the fete in 1969 and drafted a constitution for the Church. Christine had formed a committee for Wives Group and ran a working party at home.)

Informed by architect Mr Derek Walden, we are able to go out to tender. Donations totalling £350 received towards Building fund.

13th July. Summer fete on Meadgate School sports field, with music by Chelmsford Silver Band.
September. The Pastoral Committee made a further grant of £2,000 on top of interest free loan.

Time Line

1971

February. More small donations received. We now had £5,000 on deposit. £6,000 promised from Diocese.

March. An hour of prayer for the work on Meadgate by invitation of Dr. J Houghton at her home.

4th July. Plans completed by architect Mr Derek Walden. Builders invited to tender for the construction of the church. More donations and gifts of equipment for the centre received.

12th September. Tender accepted of £15,782 for the building of the Church Centre by builders AN Hill. Professional fees and cost of furnishings added. Interest free loan of approximately £14,000 promised. To be free of debt £7,000 needed.

24th October. Cutting the turf ceremony on the building site. Builders then began work, hoping to complete work in eight months.

1972

During this year till beginning of 1973 a legal committee from all three of the Great Baddow churches discussed a new constitution for the parish and each of the churches, allowing for Meadgate Church to reflect its ecumenical beginnings and vision.

2nd February. Reception at Meadgate School to present plans for the purpose of the new church centre to local residents - attendance of nearly 200.
First deacons appointed: Mrs Mary Barton, Mr Dick Crossley, Mr Terry Gilder, Mr Bill Hill, Mr Melvyn Sach.

18th June. Opening of the new church centre building and dedication of the new church by the Right Reverend Neville Welch, Bishop of Bradwell assisted by the Revd MS Stedman, curate, and the Revd J. A. Kingham, rural dean and rector of St Mary's, Great Baddow.

Sunday School numbers: 20 Beginners, 50 Primaries, 80 Juniors.
Sunday morning service attendance: Ordinary 40, Family Services 150 -180.

September. Playgroup on weekdays opened for pre-school children, ran by Mrs Betty Mead and four trained helpers. Number of children attending rose to 20 by the end of the year.

Time Line

16th to 24th September. the Revd John Goldigay arrived with a team of students from St John's College, Nottingham and led an evangelistic mission ('Meet the Men for the Ministry') in the area.

October. Some Meadgate participation in a Chelmsford mission called 'Choose Freedom'.

Autumn Fair.

1973

15th April. Departure of the Revd Michael Stedman and family to Norfolk.

Arrival of new curate the Revd Tony Bishop with wife Pat and children Jonathon and Christopher.

Holy Communion order of service changed from 'Eucharist for the Seventies' to 'Series Three.'

26th August. First church service at Meadgate by Tony Bishop.

October. Commemoration of 10th year anniversary of Meadgate Church with Autumn Fair, Harvest Supper and Parish Evangelism Course.

16th December. Carol Service with the Rt Revd John Trillo, Bishop of Chelmsford.

1974

Original Meadgate committee disbanded and replaced by elected deacons, the first being Clive Abbot (treasurer), Mary Barton (secretary), Marion Bishop, Terry Gilder, Bill Hill and Melvyn Sach.

July. Sunday School trip to Walton-on-the-Naze and picnic.

July. Percy and Joyce Walden take on caretaking duties.
Started using Scout hut for some Sunday school activities.

August. First funeral service at Meadgate Church for Mrs Florence Day, a faithful member of the congregation.

1975

Continued use of Scout hut and also Meadgate School hall for Sunday school use.

January - February. Clive Calver's evangelism team 'In the Name of Jesus' at Meadgate, including singer/songwriter Graham Kendrick.

June. 'Buy-a-Brick' building fund raising scheme ran by Mr and Mrs Keeble ended.

Time Line

19th October. Baptism by immersion of Gail Bridges in joint service at Springfield Park Baptist Church.

21st December. Christmas Carol Service.

1976

October. Outdoor Family Service at Meadgate School playing field, singing by Maranatha music group from St Mary's.

17th December. Christmas Carol Service.

1977

Apart from Sunday services regular activities running at this time were: Sunday School, Pathfinders group, Wayfinders, Senior Citizens, Wives group, several house groups, and a weekday playgroup for pre-school children.

January. Departure of Tony Bishop and family for him to engage in church work in Nigeria.

February. Arrival of new curate the Revd John Adams and wife Anna.

April. Departure of Terry and Beryl Gilder and their children as he took up a post of headmaster at a school in Suffolk. Tom Smith-Hughes filled Terry's place as deacon.

New Music group set up under Russ Cooper.

5th June. Anniversary tea and service in the church.

June/July Discussions about introducing the Ministry of Healing at Meadgate. (It had been introduced at St Mary's some time previously.)

3rd July. Presentation to the Gilder family in recognition of their service to Meadgate Church before they leave the area.

12th November. Autumn Fayre in the church.

All outstanding debts on the building were paid off.

20th and 21st December. Carol singing group went round the estate.

1978

Good Friday. First representation of Meadgate Church in the Chelmsford 'March of Witness', culminating in a service at Chelmsford Cathedral.

Time Line

28th April. Church Growth Seminar at Meadgate led by Derek Cook.

15th July Family outing to Walton-on-the-Naze.

August. Start of several months of discussions to revise Meadgate Church constitution to bring it into line with the Church of England, while still retaining its ecumenical roots.

September. Wayfinder group affiliated to the Church Youth Fellowship Association (CYFA), a national organisation.

18th October. Showing of film 'Behind the Hiding Place' in the church.

2nd December. Christmas Fayre in the church.

Amplifiers and two speakers purchased and fitted in the church.

1979

Lent. Showing of the TV film 'Jesus of Nazareth' weekly up till Easter.

Beginning of monthly Sunday visits to St John's Hospital, Ward J9, immediately after morning service by a team of volunteers from Meadgate Church.

17th March. Barn Dance. Caller Mr Eric Manning.

22nd April. Dr Josephine Houghton was speaker at the Sunday morning service, following a trip to Chile to see her sister Felicity. This connection led to a long interest in the church in South America among members of Meadgate Church.

May. Percy Walden memorial lectern completed and put to use in the church.

July. Production of a widely distributed 'Reach Out' news and views magazine.

8th July. Visit of the 'Covenant Players' drama group.

31st August. Arrival of student Stephen Nolan of London Bible College on a study visit until 23rd September.

9th September. Church picnic lunch at 'Greenwoods', Stock.

14th October. Speaker from All-Nations College to introduce events of the 1980 'Meet Jesus Campaign'.

16th December. Morning 'Toy Service'.
23rd December. Evening service of Nine Lessons and Carols.

Time Line

1980

Plans for extension of curate's house submitted to Borough Council.

Proposed programme of activities to raise funds for the extension: April - Teenage Disco, May - Sponsored Walk, June - Saturday morning market at the church, July - Garden Party, October - Barn Dance, November - Christmas Market, December - Concert/ Pantomime.

January. Second copy of 'Reach Out' magazine produced.

27th January. Morning service speaker Mr Ron Spillard on forthcoming 'Meet Jesus Mission'.

30th March. Last Sunday service led by the Revd John Adams, preacher Stuart Harris, president of European Christian Mission (ECM). John and his family left for him to join ECM and subsequently to take up a post at a radio station in Italy broadcasting to East European countries under communist rule.

Meadgate Church 'Prayer Partners' scheme began.

7th - 14th June. Team of students from All-Nations Christian College came to help with a programme of events for the 'Meet Jesus Mission'.

14th June. Morning of prayer and gifts, then picnic at Hylands Park.

15th June. Anniversary Sunday, with the Revd David Evans at the morning service and the Revd Canon Jack Kingham at the evening service.

21/22nd June. Visit of students from All-Nations College.

22nd June. Arrival of new curate Peter Nicholson, wife Diane and children Sarah and Tracy.

29th June. Parish open air service, Great Baddow village.

1981

February. Completion of extension to curate's house at 55 Longfield Road.

March New church constitution completed and presented to parish PCC for ratification.

Introduction of 'Guest Services' and a new Wednesday evening group for children called 'Club 45'.

November. Eight young members of Meadgate Church confirmed at St Mary's.

Time Line

24th December. Introduction of Christmas Midnight Communion service at Meadgate.

Organisations listed as receiving donations from Meadgate Church this year: Pathfinders/CPAS, CYFA, Tear Fund, European Christian Mission, Bible Society, The Shaftesbury Society, Christian Aid, SAMS, CMS.

1982

10th January. Retirement of Canon Jack Kingham as rector.

12/13th June. Tenth anniversary of opening of the church building and visit of the Revd Michael Stedman.

27th June. Ecumenical evening service at Meadgate, led by the Revd Peter Nicholson with participation of the Revd Francis Hastings, the Revd Robert Lens van Rijn, Ann Windsor (RC), Eric Brigham (URC), Karen Locker (C of E).

'Link' group started for 14 to 16 year olds.

7th September. The Revd Jim Spence installed as new parish rector at St Mary's.

October. Harvest Supper with entertainment by 'People of the Green' music group.

6th November. Christmas Fair.

28th November. Seven Meadgate Church members confirmed at St Mary's.

1983

12th March. Barn Dance.

Negotiations with Chelmsford Council to acquire disused sheds behind the church and convert them for Sunday school use.

September. Monthly 'Men's Fellowship' meetings started.

October. Harvest Thanksgiving service with talk by John and Anna Adams.

1984

Six home-based 'Cell Groups' began.

Mission England campaign included many events across Chelmsford area and at churches, including Meadgate, which offered trips to the Billy Graham event at Ipswich football stadium.

Time Line

May. Two walled-mounted flower stands fitted. Purchased with a donation from Mr Christopher in memory of his late wife Chris.

28th May. Meadgate church ramble and picnic, from Maldon to Meadgate along the river bank.

Men's Fellowship meetings discontinued due to lack of support.

September. Return visits from the Revd Michael Stedman and the Revd John Adams.

Work began on the planning and alterations to sheds behind the church for use in church activities.

1985

21st April. Work on converting storage sheds completed. Tape ceremonially cut by Mrs Doris Hill and the refurbished building officially opened by the Revd Jim Spence.

July. Opening of neighbourhood Youth Club at Meadgate Church, weekly on Tuesday nights.

19-20th July. 'Ministry, Gifts and the Kingdom', conference at Meadgate Church on how to use the Spiritual Gifts in the work of the local church, led by the Revd John Leach and the ministry team from North Walsham.

7th September. First (and last?) inter-church cricket match for the 'Baddow Ashes' (a small pot containing ashes of the old St Mary's parish hall). A team of Meadgate Church members played a team from St Mary's at Marconis Sports field. Meadgate won.

8th September. Church picnic at Stock.

5th October. Harvest Supper.

8th November. Night of prayer 10pm to 6am, in church.

10th November. Guest night service, including sketch 'The Price is Paid' written by Allan Bell.

24th November. Confirmation of 14 young people from Meadgate at St Mary's.

31st December. New Year's Eve party in church.

Time Line

1986

Youth Club/drop-in opened Tuesday nights led by Jeff Hill and Peter Wyatt.

7th September. Church picnic at Stock.

12th-28th September. Major involvement by Meadgate in inter-church 'Mission Chelmsford' events in Chelmsford organised by the Revd Daniel Cousins, diocesan evangelist.

18th October. Barn Dance in church.

15th November. Meadgate Church social, meal and entertainment.

23rd November. Nine Meadgate Church members confirmed at St Mary's.

19th December. Youth disco in Church.

21st December. Evening Nine Lessons and Carols service.

31st December. New Year's Eve party in Church.

1987

1st May. Service and Act of Dedication for the Inauguration of the Great Baddow Team Ministry, led by the Bishop of Bradwell.

4th May. May Fair Parade. Large team from Meadgate gave a performance based on Graham Kendrick's 'Make Way' songs at Baddow Recreation ground.

14th June. 15th Anniversary Service, including an 'Act of Dedication and Thanksgiving', preacher the Revd Canon Jack Kingham.

18th July. Combined parish celebration evening at St Mary's. Meadgate presented a play called 'Frankie Stein', written by Allan Bell and directed by Jeff Hill, with a cast of seven.

6th September. Meadgate Church picnic at Greenwoods House, Stock.

26th September. Harvest Supper and Barn Dance.

1st October. Meetings at 1.15pm and 8.00pm to study aspects of healing ministry, including Bishop David Pytches' video 'Authority and Power'.
31st October. Pathfinders put on an 'alternative Halloween' Praise Party.

5th November. Visit from the Prophetic Word Ministry team.

Time Line

14th November. Christmas Fayre in Church.

13th December. Team from Meadgate Church lead the Sunday morning service in the chapel of Chelmsford Prison. Arranged with the chaplain Geoff Hayward by Allan Bell, who gave an introduction and led prayers; sermon by Jeff Hill, song group led by Peter Wyatt on guitar. Meadgate Church carol service in the evening.

31st December. New Year's Eve party in Church including panto 'Mac in the Beanstalk'.

1988

10th January. Meadgate music group team starts monthly Sunday morning after-service visits to patients in St John's hospital, to provide fellowship, a brief talk and some hymns.

18th January. Inter-Church fellowship AGAPE service at Meadgate.

30th January. Day of prayer for youth work at Meadgate.

24th February. Barn Dance in Church, caller Mr Eric Manning.

28th February. Moving On Praise party and farewell to Mark and Jenny Philips and their sons, off to New Zealand.

1st March. Meadgate Church became a district church within Great Baddow Team Ministry, with St Mary's and St Paul's. The minister, the Revd Peter Nicholson, was now a Team Vicar. The committee was now termed Meadgate District Church Committee (MDCC) and included two Church Wardens, but also retained two Elders. First elected MDCC members were: Clive Abbot, June Davidson, Roy Davidson, Stan Gill, Bill Hill, Melvyn Sach, Jill Smith-Hughes, Brian Smith and Judith Whalley.
Post of Vice-chairman created to stand in for the vicar at meetings and to assist the two elders in day-to-day matters of the church. First occupant Mr Clive Abbot. Elders (selected by vicar): Bill Hill and Melvyn Sach.

12th March. Quiz Evening, fund-raising event.

31st March. Maundy Thursday Agape supper based on Jewish Passover meal.

2nd May. Street parade and May Fayre in association with other local churches and organisations at Baddow Recreation Ground. Victorian theme with a Meadgate float.

Time Line

2nd July. Chelmsford Carnival. Meadgate Church participated along with other churches in the area, theme: 'Crown of thorns to crown of glory. Jesus is alive'.

4th July. Church picnic at Hylands Park.

27th November. Four from Meadgate confirmed at St Mary's.

30th November. Jeffrey Hill commissioned as first Meadgate Church Evangelist at 10am. service. 8pm. Extraordinary open Church meeting to 'discuss and approve a new church constitution'.

18th December. Carol Service, nine lessons, coffee and mince pies.

31st December. New Year's Eve informal drop-in party at the new vicarage.

1989

February. Began serving tea and coffee after church services.

23rd February. Formation of a door-to-door evangelism team by Jeff Hill.

11th March. Meadgate production of 'Glory Story' in Great Baddow parish hall.

22nd April. Trivial Pursuit, quiz evening with proceeds to Archbishop's Urban Fund.

1st May. Great Baddow May Fayre at Recreation Ground with presentation of the 'Glory Story' by Meadgate Church.

9th June. Meadgate Church night of prayer.

24th July. Barbecue party at Mrs Diane Chasmer's home on Baddow Road.

24th August. Praise party social event and meal in the church to celebrate the 25th wedding anniversary of the Revd Peter Nicholson and Diane.

16th September. Participation in national March for Jesus event in London.

7th October. Harvest Supper, including drama 'Casablanca' written by Allan Bell and starring John Nightingale and Lesley Bragg.

18th November. Christmas Fayre in the Church, profits to the Church Urban Fund.

18th December. Christmas Toy service.

24th December. Midnight Communion service.

25th December. Christmas Day family service

31st December. Drop-in party at vicarage.

Time Line

1990

Tony Pugsley welcomed to Meadgate Church for several months as part of his ministry training programme, with opportunities to preach, lead services and prayers, commented (in New Life, March issue): 'you have more variation of service than most churches and this has given me more experience than I could have had elsewhere.'

January. First edition of 2-monthly Youth Club magazine 'Livewire', editor: Gill Brand.

10th February. Day of prayer for children and youth.

21st February. Barn Dance, caller Mr Eric Manning, followed by a fish and chip supper.

May. New welcome pack produced: 'Meadgate Church. We believe ....'

10th June. Family Fun Day followed by Evening Service at East Mersea.

15th September. Meadgate participation in 'March for Jesus' through Chelmsford.

6th October. Harvest Supper and barn dance.

31st October. 'Son Light', alternative Halloween party.

24th November. Christmas Fayre.

23rd December. Carol Service at church preceded by carol singing tour of the estate.

1991

30th June. Church Fun Day at Gt Wenham (near Ipswich).

5th October. Harvest Supper, meal and Barn Dance.

Closure of the preschool Play Group.

22nd December. Carol Service with nine lessons.

1992

February. Installation of a deaf loop in the main hall. Temporary suspension of the Youth Club.

Time Line

4th May. Baddow May Fayre at Recreation ground, including a church marquee with Meadgate participation.

21st June 20th Anniversary, 10 am Family Worship, Leader the Revd Peter Nicholson; the Revd Canon Jack Kingham preached on the theme of Celebration and Recommitment, 1Peter 2, verses 1 to 10.

3rd October. Harvest Supper.

31st October alternative Halloween party at Meadgate Church.

13th December. Carol singing around the Meadgate Estate.

1993

30th May. 'Jam Session' youth service, speaker Phil Loose.

12th June. March for Jesus in Chelmsford, with major Meadgate participation.

December. Music group sang carols in the Beehive pub and gave away 30 copies of J. John's booklet 'What's the Point of Christmas'.

1994

Joint Alpha course with St Paul's and Galleywood churches held at Meadgate.

2nd May. May Fayre at Baddow Recreation Ground, Meadgate participation in church marquee.

October. Alternative Halloween Party attended by 65 children.

19th November. Christmas Fayre.

18th December. Carol Service.

21st December. Music Group went carol singing in Beehive pub.

December. Burglary over Christmas with theft of equipment from the church office.

1995

January to May. Great Baddow 'Festival of Faith' with events at various locations.

19th February. Special Sunday evening service with the Revd, Trevor Jones of St Mary's Widford teaching on charismatic gifts.

25th February. 'Festival of Faith' event 'Prayer Concert' at Meadgate Church.

Time Line

5th March. Meadgate School hall used for enlarged family service, including uniformed groups.

April. AGM set up a Social Events Committee under Allan Bell to plan a quarterly series of events for church and non-church people.

23rd April. Evening 'Healing Service' led by the Revd Trevor Roper and his prayer team.

20th May. Social events: walk along the river followed by a meal and entertainment in Meadgate Church.

18th June. Meadgate Church anniversary service.

2nd July. 'Sunday Live' service in Meadgate School.

7th October. Social Event: '1940s Evening' in the church.

25th November. Social Event: '1960s Evening' in the church.

10th December. Sunday morning service led by the Right Revd Laurie Green, Bishop of Bradwell.

1996

Meadgate Church operated a charity shop in the shop next door (since taken over by Chelmsford Coop.).

27th January. Social Event: '1970s Evening' in the church.

25th May. March for Jesus in Chelmsford

16th June. Social event. Picnic at Hylands Park after morning service at Meadgate Church.

2nd July. 'Meadgate Live' family service in Meadgate School.

2nd September. Harvest Supper.

September. Peter and Diane Nicholson left Meadgate for Westcliff, farewell party at the church.

7th November. Social Event, Senior Citizens open to all.

1997

8th February. Social Event in church with entertainment by local performers.

Time Line

The Social Events Committee was disbanded. A team called 'Make a Difference' (MAD) was set up to explore new ways of furthering evangelism and participation in the activities of the church.

6th December. Autumn Fair in church.

14th December. Name of new vicar announced: the Revd Mones Farah.

December. Usual Christmas Carol Service did not take place in this interregnum year, although there were Christmas Eve and Christmas Day services.

1998

26th February. Licensing service for the new vicar, conducted by the Bishop of Chelmsford.

28th February. Saturday evening of 'Fun, Fellowship and Worship', with the Revd Mones Farah, his wife Sally, and daughters.

March. A spate of petty vandalism over the past year was followed by a burglary and loss of computer equipment.

28th March. Palm Sunday, 'March for Jesus' event round Meadgate Estate.

30th April. Sponsored walk organised by Mike Fisher.

Electronic keyboard replaced an electric organ, which was sent to Romania.

Sunday evening service brought forward to 5.30pm and introduction of a third service, 'Time for Reflection, more orientated towards charismatic worship and singing of choruses.

3rd October. Harvest Supper.

December. Sunday morning carol service.

1999

'Manna Clan' group for 14 to 18 year olds joined up with 'Genesis' group at St Mary's to form a new inter-church group called 'Fuse'.

A Friday evening 'Youth Drop' was started.

Group for 9 to 14 year-olds set up, called 'Victory Warriors' and specialising in puppet entertainments.

Time Line

Church 'Fun Day' at Hazeleigh., home of the Chasmer family.
November. VIZ volunteer Andy Davis came to help with children's groups and youth 'Drop-in'.

2000

February. Youth 'Drop-in' suspended due to bad behaviour of some of the young people.

6th April. AGM meeting included presentation of plans for proposed church extension and refurbishment.

July. Pre-school weekday group ended after 28 years because of decrease in numbers, increase in regulations and departure of leader Claire Smith to study at Moorland's College.

30th September. Harvest Supper in Meadgate Church.

Beginning of a morning pre-service prayer meeting led by prayer coordinator Mrs Diane Chasmer.

December. Christmas Carol service.

2001

18th March. Start of Sunday services in Roman Catholic church building while the work on refurbishing and rebuilding Meadgate Church is carried out.

18th April. Open to all event 'An evening with Reona Peterson Joly' (Christian author) arranged by Meadgate Cameo group but held at St Mary's.

17th June. Fun day at Hazeleigh, including a service with the the Right Revd Laurie Green, Bishop of Bradwell, preaching.

27th June. Harp recital by Lyn Creasey, arranged by Meadgate Cameo at St Mary's.

October. Meadgate Church building re-opened.

23rd December. Family Carol service with puppet show by Victory Warriors in the morning and Carol Service with nine lessons in the evening.

2002

16th February. Valentine's barn and line dance.

6th April. Evening fund raising event with rock 'n roll band.

Time Line

16th June. Celebration of church's 40th anniversary, congregation lunch in church.

19th June. Cameo fund raising event: 'Marianne's Fashion Show'.

26th June. Burglary at church. Vicar plus eight lay members went to Chorleywood for a seminar on preaching, addressed by Dr Martin Sanders, internationally renowned writer and lecturer on leadership and preaching.

6th October. Harvest Service in morning, Harvest Supper in evening.

7th October. Start of 'Connect' group, follow up to Alpha course'.

30th November. Christmas Fayre in Church.

December. Christmas service with nine lessons and carols.

2003

15th February. Barn dance in the church.

29th March. Concert by Marilyn Baker, Christian singer/songwriter.

8th June. Fun day at Hazeleigh.

Autumn Edition of Baddow Life, Issue 1, the first of a free quarterly parish newspaper. Contained an article on the 40th anniversary of Meadgate Church.

2nd November. Sunday 40th Anniversary celebration service and lunch at the church.

2004

8th May. Evening Auction of donated small items in the church.

16th May, Sunday. Visit of the Right Revd Kewasis Nyorsok (Stephen), Bishop of Kitale, Kenya, who preached at the morning service, attended by Canon Philip Price and his wife Grace who were missionaries in Kenya; in retirement they became local residents and members of Meadgate Church. Baddow Life Issues 4 and 5 contain accounts of the Price's work in Kenya and meeting with the young boy who is now bishop of Kitale.

22nd August. Meadgate Community Fun Day, around car park and in church.

16th September. Mark Petitt formally appointed Church Youth Minister.

10th October. Harvest Festival service, donation of gifts to 'Harvest for the Hungry'.

Time Line

7th November. Preaching workshop.

21st November. Preaching Workshop.

19th December. Carol Service.

2005

Licence to continue as Team Vicar for a further 7 years granted to the Revd Mones Farah.

Beginning of Oasis, once a month Saturday morning café project.

April. Formalisation of the Prayer Ministry Team (who are available for prayer ministry after Sunday morning services), with a weekly rota and regular training events.

17th July. Fun day at Hazeleigh.

4th September. Second Meadgate Community Festival around car park and in church.

8th October. Harvest Supper party in Church.

9th October. Harvest Festival service, donation of gifts to 'Harvest for the Hungry'.

13th to 15th October. Meadgate Church hosts a 'Soaking Prayer Conference', with Toronto Christian Fellowship visitors.

16th December. Outdoor carol singing.

18th December. Senior Citizen's tea party followed by 5.30 Carol Service.

2006

January Portacabin for youth work installed behind the church.

January - February. Visit to Meadgate and St Paul's of nine young people from YWAM discipleship training school, Argentina. They decorate the Portacabin, help with a youth-work double-decker bus at St Paul's, work in School assemblies and with church youth groups.

26th February. The Right Revd Laurie Green, Bishop of Bradwell, preached at the morning service.

March - April. Introduction of '40-Days of Purpose' course, and setting up of a new prayer ministry team by Sally Farah.

Time Line

Effort to obtain use of the 'Army and Navy' public house for a temporary youth outreach centre.

9th July. Church fun day at Hazeleigh.

Launch of Meadgate Church website (www.meadgatechurch.org.uk) constructed by a church team led by Caroline Goatly and John Hom.)

2nd November. Christmas Fair.

17th December. Senior Citizen's tea party followed by 5.30pm Carol Service

2007

19th March. Opening of Monday morning coffee shop in side hall as part of outreach to the community. Volunteer preparation and serving team led by Mrs Diane Chasmer.

1st July. Peter Wyatt's ordination service at Chelmsford Cathedral followed by a party at Meadgate. Before training at Nottingham he had been at Meadgate for many years involved in the Music Group and Youth Work.

September to July. First 'Discipleship Training' course, ending with a visit to Israel.

7th October. Harvest Festival service and lunch in church, donation of gifts to Harvest for the Hungry.

Effort to obtain use of the 'Army and Navy' public house for a temporary youth outreach centre seemed to be proceeding well, but then the owners withdrew the offer.

19th December. Christmas lunch for senior citizens at which Mrs Irene Duke (Rene), having organised the Senior Citizens/Thursday club since 1985 formally handed over the leadership role to Mrs Sue Marriott.

2008

February. Soaking conference at Meadgate with 'Catch the Fire' ministry team.

5th March. Gospel Concert evening with George Hamilton IV, arranged by CAMEO.

Easter. Visit of YWAM Outreach team, helped with holiday club.

July. Meadgate Summer Festival in church and around car park.

August. About 30 young people from Meadgate went to the 'Soul Survivor' event.

Time Line

September to July. Start of another 'discipleship training' course now renamed Meadgate 'School of Ministry (SOM)'.

20th December. Meadgate Christmas Festival in church and around car park. Plus Nine Lessons and carols service afterwards.

2009

January. Meadgate 'School of Ministry' (SOM) team with a weekend evangelistic trip to Letterstone, Wales

17th January. Men's Breakfast group trip to Calais/Le Touquet.

4th April. Preaching Workshop.

29th May. Quiz Night.
    SOM team visit to Israel.

Launch of a youth/children's work website.

Meadgate Summer Festival in the church and around the car park.

Project for maintenance of planters (walled in flower beds around car park), one by Meadgate school, two by local residents, two by Meadgate Church under supervision of James Knights.

Mark and Lydia Petitt moved to Bristol for him to study for ordination. Mark was Youth Minister at Meadgate since 2004 and Lydia did the ALPHA and SOM courses and served as district visitor, in women's ministry and family work.

17th to 18th October. 24 hours of prayer event in the church, from 9am Saturday to 9am Sunday.

19th December. Meadgate Christmas Festival in church and around car park.

2010

May. Visit from American SERVE Nazareth team on a training programme before leaving for 3 months in Israel on 31st May.

18-19th June. 'Fresh Rain', a conference led by Lori Lawlor and Chris Finn at Meadgate Church.

4th July. Meadgate Festival, around car park and in church, following short morning service.

Time Line

23rd July. Meadgate School of Ministry (SOM) team visit Jerusalem and Nazareth, linking up with the American team.

29th August. Church 'Fun Day' at Hazeleigh.

28th September. Meadgate Church start 10-session ALPHA course at the Queen B pub.

18th November. Visit to Meadgate of Home Secretary Theresa May on a 'meet the local community' tour.

18th December. Meadgate Christmas Festival in church and around car park, plus 'Rocking Carols'.

Decade Round-Up

Regular church events and activities during the years since 2000 were:

Sundays. Three services in the Church main hall: Family Service with once a month Communion (and occasional Baptisms) at 10.30 am (preceded by a 'Soaking' session and preparatory prayers for the Ministry Team), Evening Service with once a month Communion at 5.30 pm, and Celebration Worship Service with Youth Band, 7.30 pm to 8.45 pm.

Mondays. Coffee Shop (drinks and light snacks prepared and served by church team of volunteers) in side hall 8.45 am to 12.30 pm, since 2007.
Victory Warriors (ages 11 to 14), 5pm to 6.30pm.
God Slot (ages 11 to 14), 6.30 pm to 7 pm.
Soaking, worship and healing, 8 pm to 9.30pm.

Tuesday. First Steps toddler group, 10am to 12am (since 2002).
Youth Band practice, 7pm to 8.15pm.
Fuse group (ages 14 to 18) 7.30pm to 8.30pm.

Wednesday. Holy Communion service, 10.30 am to 11.15 am (once a month)
Worship drop-in, 12.30pm to 4pm.
Music group rehearsal for Sunday morning service, 8.30pm
CAMEO ladies social group, 8pm to 10pm (fortnightly).

Thursday. Thursday Club, social event for over 60s (2pm to 3pm).

Friday. Intercessory prayer meeting, 10.30am to 12am.
Six Pack club (ages 6 to 11), 6pm to 7.15pm.

Time Line

Saturday. Men's Breakfast, 8.15am to 10.15am, once a month.
Oasis café, drinks and snacks to 'full English' breakfast, prepared and served by a team of volunteers, 10.30 am to 1.30pm, once a month.
Worship drop-in, 12.30pm to 4pm, once a month.

Other activities.
There were regular meetings of Meadgate DCC committee, with representatives at meetings of the Parochial Council and Deanery Synod, the year concluding with compilation of an annual report and accounts, open for explanation and discussion with the congregation at the AGM in April.
The Prayer Ministry team was available for ministry at the Sunday services and held regular training sessions on Saturday afternoons.
The Church Prayer Chain operated a telephone contact service for individuals or events as communicated to its members.
House groups, about ten or more, have functioned throughout the decade at times to suit members' convenience, usually following Bible study courses and sometimes providing teams to help with specific activities.
ALPHA courses continued to be a feature in the activity of the church, as well as courses for married or about-to-be married couples.
The School of Ministry continued the courses started in 2007, each course usually concluding with a trip to Israel.
There were usually specific seasonal events scheduled around Christmas and at Easter church members joined in the Chelmsford 'March of Witness', where churches around Chelmsford walk to a service in the town centre, and the church has had an annual fun day at the Hazeleigh home of the Chasmer family.
A number of seminars, talks and entertainment events were held at the church and church members regularly attended events elsewhere, such as 'Soul Survivor' for young people.
Naturally the vicar carried out the usual functions of a church minister: funerals, baptisms and marriages, aided by lay pastoral visitors, church office administrators and maintenance teams, as well as the two church wardens, team of lay preachers, readers and prayer leaders, sides-persons and those involved in setting up the hall and sound systems for the various events, flower arrangers, and the kitchen team.

2011

5th February. Musical entertainment evening by music teacher Jane Parker and past and present students, featuring classics, jazz and pop numbers.

February. Mission trip by members of Meadgate Church to Pendine, Wales (article in Baddow Life, Issue 31). Then there was a later visit to Israel (Photo in Baddow Life, Issue 32).

Time Line

12th March. Trip to Southwark Cathedral and Westminster Abbey by members of Meadgate Church (article in Baddow Life, Issue 31).

4th May. Meadgate Church start another 10-session ALPHA course at the Queen B pub.

22nd May. New Team Rector the Revd Canon Philip Ritchie installed at St Mary's.

29th May. Meadgate team participate with other churches in 'Church @ Car Boot Sale' at Boreham, regular weekly event in summer months.

Group from Meadgate visited Israel and did voluntary work at Nazareth hospital (article in Baddow Life, Issue 32).

Autumn Edition, Issue 32, of Baddow Life is the last. Contains articles/photos on Boreham car boot sale project and installation of the new rector.

2012

'Two Fat Men' cooking club opened, meeting every six weeks and providing cooking lessons to attenders, largely from outside the church congregation.

Meadgate Community festival with commemoration of the Queen's Jubilee; the church in partnership with local housing partnership (CHP) and other local bodies and shops.

October. Beginning of an 18-30 club, based mainly on promoting social activities for this age group.

November. Launch of a weekly 'Creative Hands' group, which gathers a mix of people from inside and outside the congregation to engage in making things, knitting, sewing, card making, etc.

9th December. Sunday, 4.30 pm Christmas Festival and Market in the church and around the car park.

10th December. Carol singing team at Newholme House care home and Tusser Court accommodation for the elderly.

15th December. Saturday, 4.30 pm, Family Christmas movie 'Miracle on 34th Street'.

2013

12th February. Pancake Evening and launch of 'Time to Pray', a 40-day Lenten course of prayer based on a booklet produced by Great Baddow Team Ministry, fulfilling a project devised by Stuart Saddler of Meadgate Church.

Time Line

13th February. Showing of the film 'Fireproof' at Meadgate Church. Free entry plus wine and nibbles.

9th March. CDEA meeting at Meadgate Church addressed by Christian author the Revd Michael Green.

31st March. Performance by 'Voxette' girls' choir from Kristinehame, Sweden.

21st April. Meadgate SOM team on a week's visit to Albania.

1st June. 'Echoes of Eternity', a conference day for men, addressed by Eric Delve.

15th June. Showing of 'Courageous', an inspirational film about the power of a father, at Meadgate Church, free entry.

16th June. As part of 50 years of Meadgate Church celebratory events Rev Tony Bishop (curate 1973 to 1977) visited and preached at the 10.30 am service, led by the Revd Mones Farah, team vicar.

28th July. Rev Sandra Southee, currently at St Mary's, Great Baddow, who was for long a member of Meadgate Church before ordination, visited and preached at the 10.30 am service.

4th August. Morning service followed by the Meadgate Summer Festival attended by the Mayor of Chelmsford.

11th August. Rev Michael Stedman (curate 1968 to 1973) visited and preached at the 10.30 am service.

18th August. The Revd Peter Nicholson (curate/team vicar 1980 to 1996) visited and preached at the 10.30 am service.

29th August. Thursday night Free Family Movie: 'Wreck it Ralph'.

1st September. Church Army Captain Jeff Hill, past youth leader and evangelist at Meadgate, visited from his current post in Oxfordshire and preached at the 10.30am service, followed displays of the various church activities and a church meal to celebrate the 50th anniversary of the church..

15th September. The Revd John Adams (curate 1977 to 1980) visited and preached at the 10.30 am service.

29th September. The Revd Peter Wyatt, past member and youth leader at Meadgate visited from his current post as vicar at St Francis' Church, South Croydon, and preached at the 10.30 am service.

Appendix A
Foundational Documents

Act of dedication 1972
Act of dedication 1988
First and second draft constitutions
Meadgate Church Constitution 1989
Meadgate Church Constitution (amended and updated)
Mission statement

MEADGATE CHURCH: ACT OF DEDICATION

(Extracted from the Order of Service for the Opening and Dedication of the New Church on Sunday 18 June 1972 at 3 PM)

The Bishop will say:
    Let this house be hallowed and dedicated, in the name of the Father, and of the Son, and of the Holy Spirit, the holy and eternal Trinity.
                  Amen
Then, turning to the people and holding his staff in his right hand, the Bishop shall say:
    By the authority committed unto us in the Church of God, we do set apart this house and whatsoever therein is dedicated by our prayers and benediction, and consecrate the same for the ministration of the holy services and mysteries of the Church. Amen.

Then shall the Bishop trace the sign of the Cross in the chancel in token that he takes possession of the ground upon which the Church stands, saying these words:
    Surely the Lord is in this place. This is none other than the house of God, and this is the gate of heaven.

The Rural Dean will say:
    O Lord Jesus Christ, in whom this Church is set apart, take the concrete and the timber, the bricks and mortar, the metal and stone, the detail and the whole: take the Architect's skill, the Builder's craft, and the workman's labour: take the sacrificial gift, large and small, from rich and poor, from old and young: take the long years' hopes, the long hours' talk and planning, and this day's swift joy.

Foundational Documents

The Congregation responds:

Take it all, Lord Christ, for all is Thine, and teach us how to use it all.

Mr Melvyn Sach:
Lord Christ, in whose service this church will discover its purpose, in whose name this church will find its authority, in whose spirit this church will find its strength, bring us together in spirit and purpose on this glad day. Humble us before Thy Cross, feed us at Thy table, nourish us by Thy truth, bring us with all our fellow-Christians into the communion of Thy spirit. Congregation: Bring us, in all we do in this church, closer to Thyself, O Saviour of the world, and in Thee closer to one another in friendship and caring compassion.

Mrs Doris Hill:
Lord Christ, when the weary come seeking rest, when the guilty come, seeking forgiveness, when the young come, brimful of life and energy, when the aged come, limping slow, when the stranger comes, seeking friendship, when the broken or disillusioned come, in search of healing and new hope.

Congregation:
Give us the secret of Thine understanding, the strength of Thy patience, Thy swift perception of human need, Thy compassion in meeting it, Thy redeeming grace to cover all men's sins.

Minister:
Lord Christ, into Thy hands we commit ourselves.

Congregation:
Ourselves, and all we have, Lord Christ, into Thy hands!

Foundational Documents

ACT OF DEDICATION
FOR THE
INAUGURATION OF THE GREAT BADDOW TEAM MINISTRY
LED BY
THE BISHOP OF BRADWELL
Sunday 1st May 1988

Bishop: We have come together to thank God for the new Team Ministry to the Parish of Great Baddow. I now invite the Clergy and People to join in an act of dedication, in which you may renew your commitment to Christ and to each other.

Rural Dean: People of God in this Parish, you are brothers and sisters in Christ and you all have a share in the ministry of our Lord. Will you seek to offer your gifts in Christ's Service in this Parish and in the fellowship of the gospel, supporting your Clergy with loyalty and prayer?

All: We will, with God's help.

Representatives of the two other churches: Members of ....Church, we are glad to share with you in the work of the gospel in this Parish. We offer to you our prayers and support, and we ask you to give us yours.

Members of ....Church: We thank you for the promise of your prayers and support. We gladly pledge our own to you, with God's help.

Bishop: May the Lord bless you and help you to be true to your promises. (All sit, except Churchwardens and Council members.)

Rural Dean: Churchwardens and Church Councillors, you have been elected to co-operate with the Clergy in the initiation, conduct and development of Church work in the Parish and Team Ministry. Will you re-dedicate yourselves to that in Christ's name?

Churchwardens and Councillors: We will, with God's help.

Bishop: May the Lord bless you and help you to be true to your promise. (All sit. The Clergy stand.)

Bishop: Clergy of this Parish, you are to be fathers to the family of God's people here, shepherds of the flock of Christ, caring for them and teaching them, bringing them to the Master, sharing with them his love and joy. You are to be their leaders and examples, remembering that Jesus taught us that he who leads must be the servant. Will you try to be and to do these things faithfully, not for your own glory but for the sake of Christ and of the people for whom he died?

Clergy: We will with God's help.

Bishop: May the Lord bless you and help you to be true to your promises.

This Act of dedication was repeated in the other two churches.

PRINCIPLES EMBODIED IN DRAFT MEADGATE CONSTITUTION

1. Assurance of Christian Policy.

2. Preservation of non-denominational basis.

3. Retention of self-determination for Church members, especially Meadgate residents.

4. Protection of Anglican financial interest.

5. Prevention of inertia of perpetual office.

6. Involvement of Church organisations in building management.

Foundational Documents

THE MEADGATE CHURCH

SECOND DRAFT CONSTITUTION

1. The Meadgate Church shall be a non-denominational fellowship of Christians in the Meadgate area of Great. Baddow, under the auspices of the Great Baddow Parochial Church Council.

2. Its objects shall be Christian worship and service relevant to the needs of the Meadgate area.

3. It's Minister shall be the Curate-in-charge appointed by the Vicar of St. Mary's Church, Great Baddow.

4. The policy of the Church and the administration of its funds shall be in the hands of a Council consisting of the Minister and his Deacons.

5. Membership of the Church shall be open to any convinced Christian willing to associate in worship and service with Members of the Church of England.

6. Application for membership shall be made to the Minister: Acceptance into membership shall be at the discretion of the Minister and Deacons and by formal reception of the Church.

7. An annual General Meeting of the Church shall be held in March at which all six Deacons shall be elected from the Church members. Four of these Deacons shall be regular communicant members of the Church of England: the remaining two may be any communicant members of the Church.

8. No Deacon shall serve for more than three years in succession: in any case two of the existing Deacons (if necessary decided by lot) shall not be eligible for re-election. After an interval of one year, any such member may stand again.

9. The Annual General Meeting shall ensure that adequate Representation of Meadgate residents is maintained on the Council.

10. The officers of the Council; shall be Chairman (the Minister), Vice-Chairman, Secretary and Treasurer. The last three shall be elected from the Deacons at the first meeting of the Council following the Annual General Meeting.

11. This Constitution may only be altered on a resolution of the Annual General Meeting (or a Special General Meeting called for the purpose), when such a resolution has been ratified by Great Baddow Parochial Church Council.

MEADGATE CHURCH CONSTITUTION

(Approved at the special church meeting held on the 30th November 1988 and ratified by the P.C.C. on the 14th February 1989)

A) GENERAL ADMINISTRATION

1. The Meadgate Church (Hereinafter called M.C.) shall be an ecumenical (interdenominational) fellowship of Christians under the auspices of the Great Baddow Parochial Church Council. (Hereinafter called the P.C.C.).

2. The Meadgate District is defined within Appendix D, or as agreed from time to time with the P.C.C.

3. The Minister of M.C. shall be the Team Vicar appointed by the Bishop and the Great Baddow Team Rector jointly, in consultation with the Meadgate District Church Council. (Hereinafter called the Council).

4. The objects of M.C. shall be Christian worship and service which is relevant to the needs of the Meadgate District. These will be determined by the Team Vicar, in consultation with the Council.

A statement of Beliefs and Aims of Meadgate Church is contained in Appendix A.

5. The policy of the M.C. and the administration of its funds shall be in the hands of the Council consisting of the Team Vicar and up to nine elected members, and if applicable the co-opted members.

Foundational Documents

6. The Council shall normally meet no less than four times a year and will be subject to any limits or constraints laid down by the P.C.C.

7. Leaders of any M.C. organisation may, either at their own request or that of the Council, attend a Council meeting to discuss matters concerning their organisations.

8. The general provisions relating to the operation of the Council are based on the Appendix 11 of the Church Representation Rules, dated 1 January 1985 and are summarised in Section D and Appendix B.

B) MEMBERSHIP OF M.C.

9. Membership of the M.C. shall be open to any baptised Christian, who* subscribes to the doctrine of the Holy Trinity, and has attained the age of sixteen years.

Applicants must complete the section of the Application Form (Appendix C) relating to the application for registration on the M.C. Congregational Register. They may also, if they wish and are eligible, complete the section of the form relating to the application for enrolment on the M.C. District Electoral Roll. Only those names entered on the District Electoral Roll may vote at the Annual Parochial Church Meeting of the Parish of Great Baddow. (A.P.C.M).

Initial acceptance into membership shall be dependent on the applicant residing in the M.C. district or having habitually attended worship at M.C. for at least six months.

Names of accepted applicants will be added to the Congregational Register, which is a list of all members of the M.C., and if appropriate also to the Electoral Roll of the M.C. District.

Each new member is given copies of the Constitution, the latest versions of the Congregational Register, and a statement of Beliefs and Aims of M.C.

10. There are usually to be three Open Church Meetings, to which all church attendees and members of the Congregational Register are invited. One such meeting shall be the Annual General Meeting (AGM) of M.C. as described below.

11. The Congregational Register and the District Electoral Roll shall be revised annually by, or under direction of, the Council. The revision shall be completed not less than 15 days or more than 28 days before the A.P.C.M. Notice of this revision shall be publicly displayed in the Church Centre 14 days prior to commencement of the revision.

9. A new Congregational Register and District Electoral Roll shall be prepared according to the procedure outlined in Appendix D based on the Church Representation Rules dated January 1985.

C) ANNUAL GENERAL MEETING (AGM)

13. The AGM shall be held not more than 42 days and not less than nine days before the A.P.C.M. The Team Vicar shall act as Chairman of the AGM. Only members can participate in the selection and election procedures, or any other voting issues which may arise.

All members shall be circulated with minutes of the previous AGM and relevant reports.

All nominated members must be of Communicant status and have been members for at least six months.

The AGM shall select members for the following positions on the P.C.C.
A) Two District Church Wardens. B) Two Deanery Synod Representatives (Three terms of office). C) Three P.C.C. representatives. These P.C.C. nominees are elected to office at the A.P.C.M.

Of the above nominees only the Deanery Synod Representatives are required to be on the Electoral Roll of the M.C. District and are ex-officio members of the P.C.C. Normally it is not essential that Deanery Synod representatives are members of the Council, but they shall be entitled to receive copies of the minutes of the Council meetings.

The District Churchwardens are ex-officio members of the Council and the P.C.C.

The AGM shall elect up to a total of seven members to the Council of which at least four members (including the District Churchwardens) should be P.C.C. nominees. If this ratio is not achieved at the AGM the so-option procedures described in section 17 shall be used by the Council at the first meeting after the AGM. The term of office shall last until the next AGM when all must stand down.

Foundational Documents

14. Nomination forms (Appendix E) for the selection of P.C.C. nominees and the election of the Council nominees will be available in the Church Centre at least two weeks prior to 8.00pm on the second Sunday before the AGM after which no nominations will be accepted.

When a form is completed, having been signed by nominee, proposer and seconder, (all of whom must be on the Congregational Register of M.C) it should be returned to the Team Vicar or in his absence one of the Churchwardens or Elders. At the first practical opportunity after receipt, the names of the accepted nominees are to be placed on a Summary Nomination Form (Appendix E) on a publicly displayed notice board.

Nominees are not identified as having been prior Council Members.

P.C.C. nominees (except District Church Wardens) are ex-officio members of the Council.

Candidates must be nominated separately for the selection for P.C.C. nomination and for election to the Council.

Candidates must be prepared to respond to questions from the congregation prior to election, these questions to be presented in writing at least three days before the A.G.M. of Meadgate Church and to be verbally responded to before the vote for representatives.

Synod representatives who resign or who are removed for any reason before their term of office expires will be replaced by candidates selected at the next Church General Meeting after resignation or removal.

15. At the AGM separate lists of P.C.C. and Council nominees are circulated for the purpose of voting. The P.C.C. nominees are selected first by the normal voting procedure. If necessary the list of Council nominees is amended should any names need to be deleted following the first election. The Council members are then elected using the amended voting slips. Appendix F is an example of a Voting List.

16. The AGM shall also nominate an auditor to be appointed at the A.P.C.M.

Foundational Documents

D) COUNCIL PROCEDURES (SEE ALSO APPENDIX B)

17. Co-opted members up to a total Council of eleven, excluding the Team Vicar, may be appointed by the Council. Co-opted members shall be deemed to have full rights as per elected members. The co-option procedure may be required in order to fulfil section 13 of this constitution.

18. At the first Council meeting after the A.G.M, or a subsequent meeting as circumstances may require, Elders will be nominated by the Team Vicar, and with the agreement of the Council be appointed. The role of Elders in M.C. is essentially to assist and advise the Team Vicar in the Pastoral needs of the Church members and citizens of the Meadgate District.

19. The Chairman of the District Council shall be the Team Vicar having responsibility for the M.C.C. or during a vacancy, the Team Rector acting jointly with a lay Vice Chairman.

20. The officers of the Council shall be the Chairman, Vice Chairman, Secretary and Treasurer. The officers shall be elected from the Council at the first Council meeting after the A.G.M or as soon as possible.

21. The Council shall, in consultation with the Electoral Roll Officer of the Parish appoint a Membership Officer who shall have responsibility for the upkeep of the Congregational Register and the Electoral Roll thus fulfilling the role of District Electoral Roll Officer.

22. The Council shall have a Standing Committee consisting of not less than five persons. The Team Vicar and District Churchwardens shall be ex-officio members of the Standing Committee, and the Council shall by resolution appoint at least two other members from among its own members.

23. The Standing Committee shall have the power to transact the business of the Council between the meetings thereof subject to any directions given by the Council.

24. This Constitution may only be altered on a resolution of the A.G.M (or Special General Meeting called for that purpose), when such a resolution has been ratified by the P.C.C.

Foundational Documents

The contents of the appendices referred to herein, except Appendix A Part 1 Beliefs, may be determined by the Council, insofar as any external authority vested in the Appendices allows.

A resolution to amend the main part of the Constitution or Part 1 of the Appendix A, requires a two thirds majority of those present and voting at the A.G.M or Extra-ordinary General Meeting.

APPENDIX A
MEADGATE CHURCH - BELIEFS AND AIMS

PART 1. WE BELIEVE:

1) In the summary of the Christian faith as stated in the Apostles and Nicene Creed.

2) In one God, Father, Son and Holy Spirit, who is creator and ruler of the Universe and has made all things for His Glory.

3) That God the Father made us and all mankind and that in his love he sent His Son to reconcile the world to Himself.

4) That for our salvation God the Son became man and died for our sins; that he was raised victorious over death and is exalted to the throne of God, as our advocate and intercessor and that he will come again as judge and saviour.

5) That God the Holy Spirit inspires all that is good in mankind; that he came in fullness at Pentecost to be the giver of life to the Church and that he enables us to grow in the likeness of Jesus Christ.

6) That the Bible is the inspired word of God and is the authority for teaching the truth, rebuking error, correction of faults and giving instruction for right living.

AIMS

PART 2. WE AIM TO:

1) Tell others about God the Father who is creator and sustainer of the universe, and has made all things for His Glory.

2) Proclaim the gospel of Jesus Christ who died for the sins of mankind, and was raised to the right hand of God as our advocate and intercessor and continues to work in us through his Holy Spirit giving power to heal and to overcome evil.

Foundational Documents

3) Encourage people to respond to the gospel in repenting from sin, in believing in Jesus as Saviour and Lord and receiving the promised gift of the Holy Spirit.

4) Love one another in Christ through the power of the Holy Spirit to effect the development of a oneness in Christ.

5) Accept one another in Christ as he accepts us in mutual respect and love.

6) Preserve the ecumenical (interdenominational) nature of Meadgate Church, providing a Centre where baptised Christians of different persuasions can unite in worship and service.

7) Welcome to Communion services all communicant members of Christian Trinitarian Churches and to provide the means by which all who may seek may become confirmed members of the Church.

8) Serve the area of Meadgate in which the Church is situated assisting the Minister in his responsibility for people of the district.

9) Provide services to the community as appropriate such as Playgroup, Senior Citizens, Babies and Toddlers, Youth Club, within the resources available.

10) Hold Church services on Sunday morning and evening, and at other times, joining together in worship, praise, prayer and song giving Glory to God, either at Meadgate or in conjunction with fellow Christians in other places.

11) Nurture and teach those young in the faith encouraging them to grow into maturity in Christ.

12) Provide teaching classes under the direction of a Youth Co-ordinator, for children and young people up to the age of 18 years.

13) Promote the high priority of prayer, individually and corporately, through prayer cells, the prayer chain and private prayer in providing the foundation for God's work.

14) Develop house groups as places of learning, fellowship and reaching out to others, in evangelism and good works, and seeking to draw people into the body of the Church.

Foundational Documents

15) Provide pastoral care through pastoral care schemes and a Care Fund, particularly for Church members who are in need.

16) Study of the word of God, the Bible, as the means to become mature disciples of Jesus, encouraging the use of daily Bible reading notes with the object of putting the word into practice as a body and individually.

17) Uphold the democratic process of election of the District Church Council to work with the minister in forming the policy and administration of all Church matters.

18) Show respect to the elected leadership and support them in prayer and endeavour.

19) Encourage the development and discovery of the Church member's God given gifts of the Holy Spirit for service and witness to build up the body of Christ.

20) Allow the Holy Spirit to develop His fruits of love, joy, peace, patience, kindness, goodness, faithfulness, humility and self control both individually and corporately.

21) Support the work of organisations such as TEAR Fund and Christian Aid in bringing relief of suffering and Christian love to those in need locally, nationally and internationally.

22) Support both prayerfully and financially, missionary work both home and overseas with particular regard to individuals and Societies who have formed direct links with Meadgate Church.

23) Resist and stand firm against the Evil One, in the name of Christ.

24) Preserve the unity of the body of Christ; to put this above self interest and endeavour; to strive to achieve unity rather than discord, resolving differences at the individual level, avoiding gossip and slander.

25) Work actively to promote unity between local Churches in fellowship and promotion of joint activities for worship, learning, evangelism, fund raising and social meetings.

Foundational Documents

APPENDIX B
GENERAL PROVISIONS RELATING TO PAROCHIAL CHURCH COUNCILS

1. Power to Call Meetings

The chairman may at any time convene a meeting of the council. If he refuses or neglects to do so within seven days after a requisition for that purpose signed by not less than one-third of the members of the council has been presented to him, those members may forthwith convene a meeting.

2. Notices Relating to Meetings

(a) Except as provided in paragraph 5 of this Appendix, at least ten clear days before any meeting of the council, notice thereof specifying the time and place of the intended meeting and signed by or on behalf of the chairman of the council or the persons convening the meeting shall be posted at or near the principal door of the M.C.

(b) Not less than seven days before the meeting a notice thereof specifying the time and place of the meeting signed by or on behalf of the secretary shall be sent to every member of the council. Such notice shall contain the agenda of the meeting including any motion or other business proposed by any member of the council of which notice has been received by the secretary.

(c) If for some good and sufficient reason the chairman, vice-chairman and secretary, or any two of them, consider that a convened meeting should be postponed, notice shall be given to every member of the council specifying a reconvened time and place within fourteen days of the postponed meeting.

3. Quorum and Agenda

No business shall be transacted at any meeting of the council unless at least five members are present thereat and no business which is not specified in the agenda shall be transacted at any meeting except by the consent of three-quarters of the members present at the meeting.

4. Order of business

The business of a meeting of the council shall be transacted in the order set forth in the agenda unless the council by resolution otherwise determine.

5. Short Notice for Emergency Meetings.

In the case of sudden emergency or other special circumstances requiring immediate action by the council a meeting may be convened by the chairman of the council at not less than three clear days' notice in writing to the members of the council but the quorum for the transaction of any business at such meetings shall be a majority of the then existing members of the council and no business shall be transacted at such meetings except as is specified in the notice convening the meeting.

6. The meeting of the council shall be held at such place as the council may direct or in the absence of such direction as the chairman may direct.

7. Vote of the Majority to Decide. The business of the council shall be decided by a majority of the members present and voting thereon.

8. Casting Vote. In the cast of any equal division of votes the chairman of the meeting shall have a second or casting vote.

9. Minutes

(a) The names of the members present at any meeting of the council shall be recorded in the minutes.

(b) If one-fifth of the members present and voting on any resolution so require, the minutes shall record the names of the members voting for and against that resolution.

(c) An approved copy of the minutes of Council meetings shall be displayed on the Church Notice Board.

10. Adjournment. Any meeting of the council may adjourn its proceedings to such time and place as may be determined at such meeting.

11. Other Committees. The council may appoint other committees for the purpose of the various branches of church work in the parish and may include therein persons who are not members of the council. The minister shall be a member of all committees ex-officio.

12. Validity of Proceedings. No proceedings of the council shall be invalidated by any vacancy in the membership of the council or by any defect in the qualification or election of any member thereof.

APPENDIX C
District Church Electoral Roll

Under Church Representation Rules as of January 1985 the following rules apply to the District Electoral Roll.

1. A lay person shall be entitled to have his name entered on the roll on completion of the Application form.

2. Subject to the provision of this rule, a persons name shall, as the occasion arises be removed from the roll if he:-

a) Dies. b) Becomes a clerk in Holy Orders. c) Signifies in writing his desire that his name should be removed. d) Ceases to reside in the parish, unless after so ceasing he continues, in any period of six months, to attend public worship in the parish, unless prevented from doing so by illness or other sufficient cause. e) Is not resident in the parish and has not attended public worship in the parish during the preceding six months, not having been prevented from doing so by illness or other sufficient cause. f) Was not entitled to have his name entered on the roll at the time when it was entered.

3. Not less than two months before the A.P.C.M in the year 1990 and every succeeding sixth year notice in the form, set out in Appendix 1 Section 3 of the Church Representation Rules (Jan 1985), shall be publicly displayed in the Church Centre and remain so for a period not less than 14 days. At every service within the 14 day period the person conducting the service shall inform the congregation of the preparation of the New Roll and Congregational Register. (Hereinafter called Lists).

4. The Council shall take reasonable steps to inform every person whose name is entered on the previous Lists that new Lists are being prepared and that if he wishes to have his name entered on the new List or Lists he must apply for enrolment or membership.

Foundational Documents

5. The new Lists shall be prepared by entering upon them the names of persons entitled to entry under Section B of the Constitution on receipt of fresh application forms.

6. After completion of the new Lists copies shall be publicly displayed in the Church Centre for not less than 14 days before the A.P.C.M.

7. The Meadgate District is defined as all the dwellings in the area bounded by the Great Baddow by-pass, Tabors Avenue (nos 35-83, 47A-94), Baddow Road (odd numbers up to Longfield Road and Longmead Avenue (up to the junction with Tabors Avenue.)

APPENDIX D

1. Nomination Form for the Position of District Churchwarden.

Nominee   Proposer   Seconder

Etc.

The position of District Churchwarden is ex-officio on the P.C.C. and Council, the Nominee will be automatically added to the list of Nominees to the Council.

2. Nomination Form for the position of Deanery Synod Member.

Nominee   Proposer   Seconder

Etc.

The position of Deanery Synod member is ex-officio on the P.C.C. and the Nominee must be on the electoral roll of the M.C. District. The Deanery Synod member is not necessarily ex ex-officio on the M.C.C.
M.C. is allowed two Deanery Synod representatives.

3. Nomination Form for position of P.C.C. Member

Nominee   Proposer   Seconder

Etc.

M.C. is allowed 3 P.C.C. Members, they are not ex ex-officio members of the M.C.C. Candidates must be nominated separately for P.C.C nomination and Council nomination. P.C.C. nominees may be required to be co-opted onto the Council.

4. Nomination Form for position of Council member.

Nominee   Proposer   Seconder

Etc.

The Council shall consist of 9 members (excluding co-opted members and the Team Vicar) of which 4 members shall be P.C.C. nominees. District Churchwardens are ex-officio members of the Council.

A summary list with the names of nominees shall be displayed publicly during the nomination procedure.

APPENDIX F
MEADGATE CHURCH VOTING LISTS
A. SELECTION OF P.C.C. NOMINEES

1. District Churchwardens. Please vote for no more than TWO CANDIDATES.

The position of District Churchwarden is ex-officio on the P.C.C. and the Council. The nominees will automatically be added to the list of nominees to the Council.

2. Deanery synod Members. Please vote for no more than TWO CANDIDATES.

The position of Deanery Synod member is ex-officio on the P.C.C and the nominee must be on the electoral roll of the M.C. district. The Deanery synod member is not necessarily ex-officio on the Council.

3. P.C.C. Member. Please vote for no more than THREE CANDIDATES.

M.C. is allowed 3 P.C.C. Members. They are not ex-officio members of the Council. Candidates must be nominated separately for P.C.C. nomination and Council nomination.

B. SELECTION OF THE COUNCIL MEMBERS

Please delete the names of the two selected Churchwardens.

Please vote for no more than SEVEN CANDIDATES.

Please note the above voting lists must be on separate sheets of paper.

APPENDIX G
ROLL OF ELDERS AND CHURCHWARDENS

1. The role of District Church Wardens is as laid out in Canon Law and other Church of England official Documents and is detailed as follows.

CANON LAW E.1 Para 4. The Churchwardens when admitted are officers of the Ordinary. They shall discharge their duties as are by law and custom assigned to them; they shall be foremost in representing the laity and in co-operating with the incumbent; they shall use their best endeavours by example and precept to encourage parishioners in the practice of true religion and to promote unity and peace among them. They shall also maintain order and decency in the church and churchyard, especially during the time of divine service.

Para 5. In the churchwardens is vested the property in the plate, ornaments, and other moveable goods of the church, and they shall keep an inventory thereof which they shall revise from time to time as occasion may require. On going out of office they shall deliver to their successors any goods of the church remaining in their hands together with the said inventory, which shall be checked by their successors.

CANON LAW E.2

Para 3. It shall be the duty of the sidesmen to promote the cause of true religion in the parish and to assist the churchwardens in the discharge of their duties in maintaining order and decency in the church and churchyard, especially during the time of divine service.

(Further information can be found in the HANDBOOK FOR CHURCHWARDENS AND CHURCH COUNCILLORS by Macmorran and Elphinstone, Published by Mowbrays).

Foundational Documents

2. THE ROLE OF ELDERS IS AS FOLLOWS:

a) To meet regularly and often with the Team Vicar for the following purposes:

i. To endeavour to provide Pastoral Care for the Team Vicar and his family.

ii. Prayer.

iii. Advise the Team Vicar on the pastoral needs of Church Members and citizens of the Meadgate District.

b) To act as "lay ministers" in pastoral care generally.

c) To assist in the leading of services and the administration of Holy Communion.

MEADGATE CHURCH CONSTITUTION
The constitution was

(Approved at the special church meeting on the 30th November 1988 and ratified by the P.C.C. on the 14th February 1989). It was amended in 1991 and updated in 2004.

A) General Administration

1. The Meadgate Church (Hereinafter called M.C) shall be an ecumenical (interdenominational) fellowship of Christians under the auspices of the Great Baddow Parochial Church Council (Hereinafter called the P.C.C).

2. The Meadgate District is defined within Appendix D, or as agreed from time to time with the P.C.C.

3. The Minister of M.C. shall be the Team Vicar appointed by the Bishop and the Great Baddow Team Rector jointly, in consultation with the Meadgate District Church Council. (Hereinafter called the Council)'

Foundational Documents

4. The objects of the M.C. shall be Christian worship and service which is relevant to the needs of the Meadgate District. These will be determined by the Team Vicar in consultation with the Council.

The statement of Beliefs and Aims of Meadgate Church is contained in Appendix A.

5. The policy of the M.C. and the administration of its funds shall be in the hands of the Council consisting of the Team Vicar and up to nine elected members, *including two Church wardens* and if applicable the co-opted members. *(Section 17).*

6. The Council shall normally meet no less than four* times a year and will be subject to any limits or constraints laid down by the P.C.C.

7. Leaders of any M.C. organisation may, either at their own request or that of the Council, attend a Council Meeting to discuss matters concerning their organisations.

8. The general provisions relating to the operation of the Council are based on the Appendix 11 of the Church Representation Rules, dated 1st January 1985 and are summarised in Section D and Appendix B

B) MEMBERSHIP OF M.C.

9. Membership of the M.C. shall be open to any baptised Christian who subscribes to the doctrine of the Holy Trinity, and has attained the age of sixteen years.

Applicants must complete the section of the Application Form (Appendix C) relating to the application for registration on the M.C. Congregational Register. They may also, if they wish and are eligible, complete the section of the form relating to the application for enrolment on the M.C. District Electoral Roll. Only those names entered on the District Electoral Roll may vote at the Annual Parochial Church Meeting of the Parish of Great Baddow. (A.P.C.M).

Initial acceptance into membership shall be dependent on the applicant residing in the M.C. district or having habitually attended worship at M.C. for six months.

Names of accepted applicants will be added to the Congregational Register, which is a list of all members of the M.C, and if appropriate also to the Electoral Roll of the M.C. district.

Each new member is given copies of the Constitution, the latest versions of the Congregational Register, and a statement of Beliefs and Aims of M.C.

10. There are usually to be three Open Church meetings, to which all church attendees and members of the Congregational Register are invited. One such meeting shall be the Annual General meeting (AGM) of M.C. as described below.

11. The Congregational Register and the District Electoral Roll shall be revised annually by, or under direction of, the Council. The revision shall be completed not less than 15 days or more than 28 days before the A.P.C.M. Notice of this revision shall be publicly displayed in the Church Centre 14 days prior to the commencement of this revision.

12. A new Congregational Register and District Electoral Roll shall be prepared according to the procedure outlined in Appendix D based on the Church Representation Rules dated January 1985.

C) ANNUAL GENERAL MEETING AGM)
13. The AGM shall be held not more than 42 days and not less than nine days before the A.P.C.M. The team Vicar shall act as Chairman of the AGM. Only members can participate in the selection and election procedures, or any other voting issues which may arise.

All members shall be circulated with minutes of the previous AGM and relevant reports.

All nominated members must be of Communicant status and have been members for at least six months.

The Council shall consist of nine members and these members of the Council shall be elected for a period of three years. After serving their term, they may stand for re-election again; however it is preferable if they have a year break and the total of consecutive years served shall not exceed 6 years, I.e. two terms of office.

The AGM shall select members for the following positions on the P.C.C. a) Two District Church Wardens. (Maximum of 6 years of office) B) Two Deanery Synod Representatives (Three year term of office). C) Three P.C.C. representatives. These P.C.C. nominees are elected to office at the A.P.C.M.

Foundational Documents

Of the above nominees only the Deanery Synod Representatives are required to be on the Electoral Roll of the M.C District and are ex-officio members of the P.C.C. Normally it is not essential that Deanery Synod representatives are members of the Council, but they shall be entitled to receive copies of the minutes of the Council meetings.

The District Churchwardens are ex-officio members of the Council and the P.C.C.

The AGM shall elect up to a total of nine members (which includes two church wardens) to the Council of which at least four members (including the District Churchwardens) should be P.C.C nominees. If this ratio is not achieved at the AGM the co-option procedures described in section 17 shall be used by the Council at the first meeting after the AGM.

14. Nomination Forms (Appendix E) for the selection of P.C.C.. nominees and the election of the Council nominees will be available in the Church Centre at least two weeks prior to 8.00pm on the second Sunday before the AGM after which no nomination will be accepted.

When a form is completed, having been signed by the nominee, proposer and seconder, (all of whom must be on the Congregation Register of M.C) it should be returned to the Team Vicar or in his absence one of the Churchwardens or Elders. At the first practical opportunity after receipt, the names of the accepted nominees are to be placed on a Summary Nomination Form (Appendix E)on a publicly displayed notice board.

Nominees are not identified as having been prior Council Members.

P.C.C. nominees (Except District Church Wardens) are not ex-officio members of the Council.

Candidates must be nominated separately for election to the P.C.C and for election to the Council.

Candidates must be prepared to respond to questions from the congregation prior to election, these questions to be presented in writing at least three days before the AGM of Meadgate Church and to be verbally responded to before the vote for representatives.

Synod representatives who resign or who are removed for any reason before their term of office expires will be replaced by candidates selected at the next Church General Meeting after resignation or removal.

15. At the AGM separate lists of P.C.C and Council nominees are circulated for the purpose of voting. The P.C.C. The P.C.C nominees are selected first by normal voting procedure. If necessary the list of Council nominees is amended should any names need to be deleted following the first election. The Council members are then elected using the amended voting slips. Appendix F is an example of a Voting list.

16. The AGM shall also nominate an auditor to be appointed at the A.P.C.M.

D) COUNCIL PROCEDURES (SEE ALSO APPENDIX B)

17. Co-opted members up to a total Council of eleven, excluding the Team Vicar, may be appointed by the Council. Co-opted members shall be deemed to have full rights as per elected members. The co-option procedure may be required in order to fulfil section 13 of this constitution.

18. At the first Council meeting after the A.G.M, or a subsequent meeting as circumstances may require, Elders will be nominated by the Team Vicar, and with the agreement of the Council be appointed. The role of Elders in M.C is essentially to assist and advice the Team Vicar in the Pastoral needs of the Church members and citizens of the Meadgate District.

19. The Chairperson of the District Council shall be the Team Vicar having responsibility for the M.C. or during a vacancy, the Team Rector acting jointly with a lay Vice-Chairman.

20. The officers of the Council shall be the Chairperson Vice-Chairperson Secretary and Treasurer. The officers shall be elected from the Council at the first Council meeting after the A.G.M or as soon as possible thereafter.

21. The Council shall, in consultation with the Electoral Roll Officer of the Parish, appoint a Membership Officer who shall have responsibility for the upkeep of the Congregational Register and the Electoral Roll, thus fulfilling the role of District Electoral Roll Officer.

22. The Council shall have a Standing Committee consisting of not less than five persons. The Team Vicar and District Churchwardens shall be ex-officio members of the Standing Committee, and the Council shall by resolution appoint at least two other members from among its own members.

23. The Standing Committee shall have the power to transact the business of the Council between the meetings thereof subject to any directions given by the Council.

24. This Constitution may only be altered on a resolution of the A.G.M (or Special General Meeting called for that purpose), when such a resolution has been ratified by the P.C.C.

The contents of the appendices referred to herein, except Appendix A Part 1 Beliefs, may be determined by the Council, insofar as any external authority vested in the Appendices allows.

A resolution to amend the main part of the Constitution or Part 1 of Appendix A requires a two thirds majority of those present and voting at the A.G.M or Extraordinary General Meeting.

APPENDIX A
MEADGATE CHURCH - BELIEFS AND AIMS
PART 1 WE BELIEVE;

1) In the summary of the Christian faith as stated in the Apostles' and Nicene Creed.

2) In One God, Father, Son and Holy Spirit, who is creator and ruler of the Universe and has made all things for His Glory.

3) That God the Father made us and all mankind and that in his love he sent His Son to reconcile the world to Himself.

4) That for our salvation, God the Son became man and died for our sins; that he was raised victorious over death and is exalted to the throne of God, as our advocate and intercessor and that he will come again as judge and saviour.

5) That God the Holy Spirit inspires all that is good in mankind; that he came in fullness at Pentecost to be the giver of life to the Church and that he enables us to grow in the likeness of Jesus Christ.

Foundational Documents

6) That the Bible is the inspired word of God and is the authority for teaching the truth, rebuking error, correction of faults and giving instruction for right living.

<u>PART 2 WE AIM TO;</u>

1) Tell others about God the Father who is creator and sustainer of the universe, and has made all things for His Glory.

2) Proclaim the gospel of Jesus Christ who died for the sins of mankind, and was raised to the right hand of God as our advocate and intercessor and continues to work in us through his Holy Spirit giving power to heal and to overcome evil.

3) Encourage people to respond to the gospel in repenting from sin, in believing in Jesus as Saviour and Lord and receiving the promised gift of the Holy Spirit.

4) Love one another in Christ through the power of the Holy Spirit to effect the development of a oneness in Christ.

5) Accept one another in Christ as he accepts us in mutual respect and love.

6) Preserve the ecumenical (interdenominational) nature of Meadgate Church, providing a centre where baptised Christians of different persuasions can unite in worship and service.

7) Welcome to Communion services all communicant members of Christian Trinitarian churches and to provide the means by which all who may seek may become confirmed members of the Church.

8) Serve the area of Meadgate in which the Church is situated assisting the Minister in his responsibility for people of the district.

9) Provide services to the community as appropriate such as Playgroup, Senior Citizens, babies and Toddlers, Youth Club, within the resources available.

10) Hold Church Services on Sunday morning and evening, and at other times, joining together in worship, praise and prayer and song giving Glory to God, either at Meadgate or in conjunction with fellow Christians in other places.

Foundational Documents

11) Nurture and teach those young in the faith encouraging them to grow up into maturity in Christ.

12) Provide teaching classes under the direction of a Youth Co-ordinator, for children and young people up to the age of 18 years.

13) Promote the high priority of prayer, individually and corporately, through prayer cells, the prayer chain and private prayer in providing the foundation for God's work.

14) Develop house groups as places of learning, fellowship and reaching out to others, in evangelism and good works, and seeking to draw people into the body of the Church.

15) Provide pastoral care through pastoral care schemes and a Care Fund, particularly for Church members who are in need.

16) Study the word of God, the Bible, as the means to become mature disciples of Jesus, encouraging the use of daily Bible reading notes with the object of putting the work into practice as a body and individually.

17) Uphold the democratic process of election of the District Church Council to work with the minister in forming the policy and administration of all Church matters.

18) Show respect to the elected leadership and support them in prayer and endeavour.

19) Encourage the development and discovery of the Church member's God given gifts of the Holy Spirit for service and witness to built up the body of Christ.

20) Allow the Holy Spirit to develop His fruits of love, joy, peace;, patience, kindness, goodness, faithfulness, humility and self control both individually and corporately.

21) Support the work of organisations such as TEAR Fund and Christian Aid in bringing relief of suffering and Christian love to those in need locally, nationally and internationally.

22) Support both prayerfully and financially, missionary work both at home and overseas with particular regard to individuals and Societies who have formed direct links with Meadgate Church.

23) Resist and stand firm against the Evil One, in the name of Christ.

24) Preserve the unity of the body of Christ; to put this above self interest and endeavour; to strive to achieve unity rather than discord, resolving difference at the individual level, avoiding gossip and slander.

25) Work actively to promote unity between local Churches in fellowship and promotion of joint activities for worship, learning, evangelism, fund raising and social meetings.

APPENDIX B

GENERAL PROVISIONS RELATING TO PAROCHIAL

CHURCH COUNCILS

1. **Power to Call Meetings:**

The chairperson may at any time convene a meeting of the council. If he refuses or neglects to do so within seven days after a requisition for the purpose signed by not less than one-third of the members of the council has been presented to him those members may forthwith convene a meeting.

2. **Notices Relating to Meetings:**

(a) Except as provided in paragraph 5 of this Appendix, at least ten clear days before any meeting and signed by or on behalf of the chairman of the council or the persons convening the meeting shall be posted at or near the principal door of the M.C.

(b) Not less than seven days before the meeting a notice thereof specifying the time and place of the meeting signed by or on behalf of the secretary shall be sent to every member of the council. Such notice shall contain the agenda of the meeting including any motion or other business proposed by any member of the council of which notice has been received by the secretary.

(c) If for some good and sufficient reason the chairman, vice-chairman and secretary, or any two of them consider that a convened meeting should be postponed notice shall be given to every member of the council specifying a reconvened time and place within fourteen days of the postponed meeting.

3. **Quorum and Agenda:**

No business shall be transacted at any meeting of the council unless at least five members are present thereat and no business which is not specified in the agenda shall be transacted at any meeting except by the consent of three-quarters of the members present at the meeting.

4. **Order of Business:**

The business of a meeting of the council shall be transacted ;in the order set forth in the agenda unless the council by resolution otherwise determine.

5. **Short Notice for Emergency Meetings:**

In the case of sudden emergency or other special circumstances requiring immediate action by the council a meeting may be convened by the chairman of the council at not less than three clear days' notice in writing to the members of the council but the quorum for the transaction of any business at such meetings shall be a majority of the then existing members of the council and no business shall be transacted at such meetings except as is specified in the notice convening the meeting.

6. The meeting of the council shall be held at such place as the council may direct or in the absence of such direction as the chairman may direct.

7. **Vote of Majority to Decide:**

The business of the council shall be decided by a majority of the members present and voting thereon,

8. **Casting Vote :**

In the cast of any equal division of votes the chairman of the of the meeting shall have a second or casting vote.

9. **Minutes:**

(a) The names of the members present at any meeting of the council shall be recorded in the minutes.

(b) If one-fifth of the members present and voting on any resolution so require, the minutes shall record the names of the members voting for and against that resolution.

(c) An approved copy of the minutes of Council meetings shall be displayed on the Church Notice Board.

10. **Adjournment:**
Any meeting of the council may adjourn its proceedings to such a time and place as my be determined at such meeting.

11. **Other Committees:**

The council may appoint other committees for the purpose of the various branches of church work in the parish and my include therein persons who are not members of the council. The minister shall be a member of all committees ex-officio.

12 **Validity of Proceedings:**

No proceedings of the council shall be invalidated by any vacancy in the membership of the council or by any defect in the qualification or election of any member thereof.

APPENDIX C

WHAT IS THE CHURCH ELECTORAL ROLL?

Why have one?

It is your Parish Church's Register of Electors; it is the list of those qualified to attend and to vote at the Annual Parochial Church Meeting where the elections take place for; a) the Parochial Church Council and b) the Parish's representatives on the Deanery Synod. Any person entitled to attend the Annual Parochial Church Meeting may raise any question of Parochial and general Church interest.

Renewal of the electoral roll takes place in 2002 and every six years thereafter. In a year of renewal no names are carried over from the old Roll and everyone must make a new application to be included on the new Roll.

What difference does it make?

Foundational Documents

By enrolling you become a voting member of the Church of England and so help to ensure that all the Synodical Councils of the Church - the Parochial Church Council, the Deanery Synod, the Diocesan Synod and the General Synod - are fully representative of its members.

Synodical government gives an opportunity for partnership between Bishops, Clergy and Laity in the life of the Church.

First, the system is intended to enable Church people at every level to be in touch with the Church as a whole and to play their part in decision making.

Secondly, the system is intended to ensure that the laity have their place in every aspect of Church life, including its Doctrine and Services.

APPENDIX C (a)

APPLICATION FOR ENROLMENT ON THE CHURCH ELECTORAL ROLL OF THE PARISH OF GREAT BADDOW

APPENDIX C (b)

APPLICATION FOR ENROLMENT ON THE CONGREGATIONAL REGISTER FOR MEADGATE CHURCH, GREAT BADDOW.

Samples of these two documents follow .

APPENDIX D

DISTRICT CHURCH ELECTORAL ROLL

Under Church Representation Rules as of January 1985 the following rules apply to the District Electoral Roll.

1. A lay person shall be entitled to have his name entered on the roll on completion of the Application Form (see Appendix C)

2. Subject to the provision of this rule, a persons name shall as the occasion arises be removed from the roll if he :-

a) Dies b) Becomes a clerk in Holy Orders. C) Signifies in writing his desire that his name be removed. D) Ceases to reside in the parish, unless after so ceasing he continues, in any period of six months to attend public worship in the parish, unless prevented from doing so by illness or other sufficient cause.

E) Is not resident in the parish and has not attended public worship in the parish preceding six months, not having been prevented from doing so by illness or other sufficient cause. F) Was not entitled to have his name entered on the roll at the time when it was entered.

3. Not less than two months before the A.P.C.M in the year 1990 and every succeeding sixth year notice in the form, set out in Appendix 1 Section 3 of the Church Representation Rules (Jan 1985), shall be publicly displayed in the Church Centre and remain so for a period not less than 14 days. At every service within the 14 day period the person conducting the service shall inform the congregation of the preparation of the New Roll and Congregational Register. (Hereinafter called Lists).

4. The Council shall take reasonable steps to inform every person whose name is entered on the previous Lists that new Lists are being prepared and that if he wishes to have his name entered on the new List of Lists he must apply for enrolment or membership.

5. The new Lists shall be prepared by entering upon them the names of persons entitled to entry under Section B of the Constitution on receipt of fresh application forms.

6. After completion of the new Lists copies shall be publicly displayed in the Church Centre for not less than 14 days before the A.P.C.M.

7. The Meadgate District is defined as all dwellings in the area bounded by the Great Baddow by-pass, Tabors Avenue (nos. 35-83,47A-94, Baddow Road (odd numbers up to*

APPENDIX E

1. Nomination form for the position of District Church Warden:

The position of the two District Churchwardens is ex-officio on the P.C.C. and Council, the Nominee will be automatically added to the list of Nominees to the council, The district Church wardens are elected annually for a one year period but not exceeding 6 consecutive years i.e. 6 terms of office.

Foundational Documents

2. Nomination form for the position of Deanery Synod Member. (3 Year Term)

Nominee   Proposer   Seconder

The position of Deanery Synod member is ex-officio on the P.C.C and the Nominee must be on the electoral roll of the M.C. District. The District Church warden are elected annually for a one year period but not exceeding 6 consecutive years I.E. 6 terms of office

3. Nomination form for position of P.C.C Member

Nominee   Proposer   Seconder.

3 Members of the M.C electoral roll are to be nominated for election annually, the district Church Wardens are ex-officio members of the DCC as well as the 2 Deanery Synod Members. Failing to elect the 3 required members the M.C.C shall make up the total required representation.

4. Nomination form for position of council member

Nominee   Proposer   Seconder

The Council shall consist of 9 members including the 2 District Church Wardens as ex-officio members, and excluding co-opted members and the Team Vicar. The elected members of the church council shall be elected for a period of three years. After serving their term they may stand for re-election again however it is preferable if they have a year break and the total consecutive years served shall not exceed 6 years i.e. two terms of office.

The Council shall consist of 9 members including the two District Churchwardens who are ex-officio members, and excluding co-opted members and the Team Vicar. The members of the Council shall be elected for a period of three years. After serving their term they may stand for re-election again, however it is preferable if they have a years break and if consecutive years are served this shall not exceed six years, i.e. two terms of office.

N.B.: In order to facilitate the start of this scheme, in the election for 2003/4 members of the Council shall be elected to a period of one, two and three years. Initially this shall be sought on a voluntary basis from the existing members of the Council should they wish to re-stand for election. However, if the circumstances still dictate a different method of decision, then the names of two nominees shall be chosen for three years, two nominees for two years and three nominees for one year, if re-standing. Any new nominee is automatically entered for a three year period, in such a situation then the number of the existing Council members seeking re-election for three years will be reduced.

....

APPENDIX F

MEADGATE CHURCH VOTING LISTS

A.　SELECTION OF P.C.C. NOMINEES

1. <u>District Churchwardens.</u> Please vote for no more than TWO CANDIDATES. The position of District Churchwarden is ex-officio on the P.C.C. and the council. The nominees will automatically be added to the list of nominees to the Council.

2 <u>Deanery Synod Members:</u> Please vote for no more than TWO CANDIDATES. The position of Deanery Synod member is ex-officio on the P.C.C. and the nominee must be on the Electoral Roll of the M.C. District. The Deanery Synod member is not necessarily ex-officio on the Council.

3. <u>P.C.C. Member.</u> Please vote for no more than THREE CANDIDATES, as M.C. is allowed three P.C.C. members. They are not ex-officio members of the Council. Candidates must be nominated separately for the P.C.C. nomination and Council nomination.

B.　SELECTION OF THE COUNCIL MEMBERS.

Please delete the names of the two selected Churchwardens.

Please vote for no more than SEVEN CANDIDATES.

Please note the above voting lists must be on separate sheets of paper.

Foundational Documents

APPENDIX G

ROLL OF ELDERS AND CHURCHWARDENS

1. The role of District Churchwardens is as laid out in Canon Law and other Church of England official Documents and is detailed as follows:-

CANNON LAW E.1 Paragraph 4: The Churchwardens when admitted are officers of the Ordinary. They shall discharge their duties as are by law and custom assigned to them; they shall be foremost in representing the laity and in co-operating with the incumbent; they shall use their best endeavours by example and precept to encourage parishioners in the practice of true religion and to promote unity and peace among them. They shall also maintain order and decency in the Church and Churchyard, especially during the time of Divine Service.

Paragraph 5: In the Churchwardens is vested the property in the plate, ornaments, and other moveable goods of the Church, and they shall keep an Inventory thereof which they shall revise from time to time as occasion may require. On going out of office they shall deliver their successors any goods of the Church remaining in their hands, together with the said Inventory, which shall be checked by their successors.

CANON LAW E.2. Paragraph 3: It shall be the duty of the Sidespersons to promote the cause of true religion in the Parish, and to assist the Churchwardens in the discharge of their duties in maintaining order and decency in the Church and Churchyard, especially during the time of Divine Service.

(Further information can be found in the HANDBOOK FOR CHURCHWARDENS AND CHURCH COUNCILLORS by Macmorran and Elphinstone, Published by Mowbrays).

2. THE ROLE OF ELDERS IS AS FOLLOWS;

To meet regularly and often with the Team Vicar for the following purposes:
    i) To endeavour to provide Pastoral Care for the Team Vicar and his family.

  ii) Prayer.

  iii) Advise the Team Vicar on the pastoral needs of Church Members and citizens of the Meadgate District.

iv) To act as "lay ministers" in pastoral care generally.

v) To assist in the leading of services and the administration of Holy Communion.

April 2004.

N.B. In order to facilitate the start of this scheme, in the election for 2003/2004 members to the council shall be elected to a period of 1, 2 and 3 years. Initially this shall be sought on a voluntary basis from the existing members of the council if they wish to re-stand for election. However if the circumstances still dictate a different method of decision, the names of 2 Nominees shall be chosen for 3 years, 2 Nominees for 2 years and 3 Nominees for 1 year if re-standing for election and any new Nominee is automatically entered for 3 years period. However if there are new nominees then the number of the existing council members seeking re-election for three years will be reduced.

APPENDIX C

APPLICATION FOR ENROLMENT ON THE CONGREGATIONAL REGISTER FOR MEADGATE CHURCH, Great. BADDOW.

(for those Members of other denominations who do not wish to enrol with the Church of England but who wish to be a member of the above named Church).

Full name..

Full Address...

....Post Code......

I declare that

1. I am a baptised member of a church of another denomination and am over 16 years of age
2. I am resident in the Parish of Great Baddow.

Foundational Documents

I am not resident in the Parish of Great Baddow but have habitually attended public worship in Meadgate Church during the period of six months prior to the enrolment.

I declare that the above answers are true and I apply for inclusion on the Congregational Register of Meadgate Church in the Parish of Great Baddow.

Signed.. Dated:........................

Notes:

1. As a member of the Meadgate Church Congregational Register and within the terms of the Constitution of the same, I am permitted to vote at the Meadgate Church Annual General Meeting.

2. I understand however, that although I can be nominated for the Meadgate District Church Council, I am unable to be nominated for the Parochial Church Council or for the office of Churchwarden or Synod Member.

SAMPLE APPENDIX C

APPLICATION FOR ENROLMENT ON THE CONGREGATIONAL REGISTER FOR MEADGATE CHURCH, GREAT. BADDOW.
SAMPLE

(for those Members of other denominations who do not wish to enrol with the Church of England but who wish to be a member of the above named Church).

Full name..

Full Address..

....Post Code..............

I declare that
1. I am a baptised member of the Church of another denomination and am over 16 years of age
2. I am resident in the Parish of Great Baddow
3. I am not resident in the Parish of Great Baddow.
But have habitually attended public Worship in Meadgate

Foundational Documents

Church in the Parish of Great Baddow.

Signed:……………………………………………..Dated…………….

Notes:-
1. As a member of the Meadgate Church Congregational Register And within the terms of the Constitution of the same, I am permitted to Vote at the Meadgate Church Annual General Meeting.
2. I understand however, that although I can be nominated for the Meadgate District Church Council, I am unable to be nominated for the Parochial Church Council or for the office of Churchwarden or Synod Member.

Meadgate Mission Statement

'Responding to and showing our love for Jesus through commitment and service. Aiming to be like him'.

Meadgate Church as Jesus' body in this place …

Seeks to be a Church that is passionately in love with God the Father, God the Son and God the Holy Spirit

Aims to go deeper in the things of God through following the Bible and the guidance of the Holy Spirit

Reveals God's love and glory to the world by reacting out to the lost, seeing broken lives healed, people encouraged, motivated and empowered to live in accordance with what God desires.

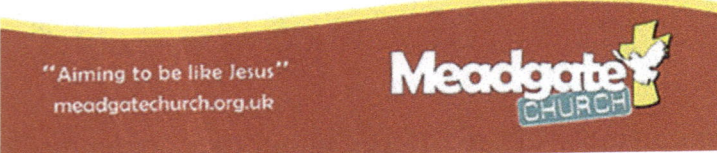

www.ingramcontent.com/pod-product-compliance
Lightning Source LLC
Chambersburg PA
CBHW081130170426
43197CB00017B/2809